Praises For
Creation Illuminated

Monique Keller takes readers on a journey of reflection and enlightenment through her book *Creation Illuminated*. She relates concepts of love, kindness, gratitude, connection, light and darkness, flow and abundance, and many more through the Creator and his creation of life. Monique's sharing of her own journey in overcoming fear and shame; of growth and finding love and acceptance, brings such depth and meaning, and palpable emotion to this beautiful narrative. She embraces her writing with the wisdom and love from the Creator and uses analogies and descriptions relating to parts of our body, like our hearts and the heartbeat our breath and our lungs, to portray her message of receiving and accepting that our Creation, and Heaven and Earth, are made in love. Through her writing, Monique helps the reader to shift their focus to a more positive outlook, bringing with it a new perspective, with a deeper understanding of life and finding meaning in why Creation is the beginning of a beautiful journey, even if there are challenges and hardships along the way. Let this book put you on a path of transformation, filled with love.

Thank you for an uplifting and powerful read Monique.

— Dr. Ingrid Sellschop

***

A powerful love story. From the beginning to the end it is all about LOVE. A message about the Creator, Yahweh, and the beauty in His creation. How nature speaks of His love and care for His ultimate creation of human beings. We are the focus, recipients, and conduits of His love. This book encourages us to see God as our creator and how His love can flow in and through our lives as a river to transform us and empower us to serve other people. I loved how the author brought the physical aspects of life with the spiritual world, the picture of God and the divine in everything "a signature of love from the Creator". This book brings to life the wonder of the human anatomy, physiology of the human body, a living miracle, loved and designed to love. This book will live you challenged to desire more of God's love in your life, live for Him, love Him wholeheartedly by loving others, and appreciating the beauty all around you.

—**Sonti Pilusa**

***

What a beautiful illustration of the creation of God. It struck my heartstrings to the wonder of how fearfully and wonderfully we were made. God is a meticulous Creator, nothing goes to waste. He uses every single piece of resource (joy, pain, disappointment, fear, and everything else) to create something out of nothing. His abundance is palpable. What an absolute honor to be called the crown of His creation. The author's deep love and appreciation for her Creator can be felt in her personal stories. As a teacher, though not vocationally, Teaching in love was a beautiful reminder for me to never underestimate the deep needs of your audience. Let love flow like a river, seeping into those cracks and brokenness that we so often do not even see in our neighbor. By doing this, we can actively participate in God's Love action plan and not merely reminisce on words spoken in the Bible.

—**Mercia Patience**

Creativity Illuminated

***

When reading ***Creativity Illuminated*** the author has a wonderful way of reminding the reader of the Creator's love for us in the magnificence and splendor of his creation. His love is life-sustaining depicted sometimes as a slow meandering stream or all-consuming tsunami to the flow of blood through our bodies ensuring our very existence. The book is a pleasure to read, linking scripture with everyday historical events as a means of presenting the book's message. In the latter part of the book the author shares ideas on how to manage obstacles that might influence one's relationship with self, others, and the Creator that readers will find helpful. I am convinced that the book will encourage readers to look at life differently and move from darkness into light supported by the knowledge of the Creator's love.

—Ronel Roos

Creation Illuminated

Monique M Keller

Published by KHARIS PUBLISHING, imprint of KHARIS MEDIA LLC.

Copyright © 2021 Monique M. Keller

ISBN-13: 978-1-63746-101-3

ISBN-10: 1-63746-101-1

Library of Congress Control Number: 2021950402

All rights reserved. This book or parts thereof may not be reproduced in any form, stored in a retrieval system, or transmitted in any form by any means - electronic, mechanical, photocopy, recording, or otherwise - without prior written permission of the publisher, except as provided by United States of America copyright law.

All New and Old Testament Scripture quotations, unless otherwise indicated, were taken from The New King James Version of the Bible. Copyright © 1979, 1980, 1982 by Thomas Nelson Publishers.

All KHARIS PUBLISHING products are available at special quantity discounts for bulk purchase for sales promotions, premiums, fund-raising, and educational needs. For details, contact:

Kharis Media LLC
Tel: 1-479-599-8657
support@kharispublishing.com
www.kharispublishing.com

Thank you Dr Ingrid Sellschop for generously sharing and allowing the use of your photographs (Creation Illuminated, Earth, Seas and Grass, herbs and fruit). To my darling, talented and nature-loving husband Paul Keller. Thank you for allowing me to use your photographs (bottom Earth, Land, Birds and Sun). Nikki Solomon thank you for your editorial support.

A life filled with the purest love from Pieter, Linda, Paul, Erin and Ross. You have calmed my spirit, and your consistent love fuels and sustains me.

CONTENTS

1. **PART I: Earth** — 1
   - Creativity in Creation — 3
2. **PART II: Land** — 9
   - The First Day Created — 11
   - The Second Day Created — 17
   - Love Created: Flow of Love in Nature — 21
   - The Third Day Created — 26
   - The Fourth Day Created — 29
   - The Fifth Day Created — 31
3. **PART III: Seas** — 35
   - Creation of Man — 37
   - The Heart — 38
   - Ego in Love — 47
   - Breath of Life — 50
   - Heartbeat — 54
   - A Heart Attack — 56
4. **PART IV: Grass, Herbs and Fruits** — 58
   - Creation of Love: Flow Affected — 60
   - Creation of Love: Overcoming Shame — 69
5. **PART V: Birds** — 78
   - Second Creation: Jesus — 80
   - Student Becomes a Teacher — 84

	Love According to Paul	90
	Love According to John	92
	Love According to Matthew	95
	Love According to Mark	98
	Love According to Luke	104
6	**PART VI: Sun**	107
	Love of the Vine	109
	Love in the Trinity	114
	Citation	117

PART I

Creativity is a skill that is sought in every industry in the world. To be able to create a product that has never been seen, used, or even disrupts the industry is what every employer wants from employees and what every creative strives to produce. The newly created idea or product can change what was once believed as possible to a new level of information, shifting humanity that little bit forward in evolving. In part I, an example of the creative Archimedes is given, culminating to the introduction of the ultimate Creator.

CREATIVITY IN CREATION

The word creation is rich with meaning and has many definitions trying to explain a complex phenomenon. It is a process where a physical or intangible object or idea is produced, which can be valuable, new, and has never been there prior to the Creation.

Creativity can be a method or idea to solve a complex problem. This requires intellectual ingenuity and complex problem-solving. Creativity can also be appreciated in easier situations, such as through play in children.

Children with a big imagination create new games to play. They have endless hours of fun. Playing is all that matters; being in the moment is key. They have no worries about what others will think of their imagination and creativity in play. They create. "Look, Mommy, look what I have made Daddy!".

Sharing their creation, be it a sandcastle that was built or a picture that was drawn or painted, someone needs to look at and appreciate the creation.

Creativity is a trait that makes humans sparkle, invent, and innovate. However, at times during "adulting," creativity slows down and, at worst, it comes to a stop. Creations that are dreamed about may never see the light of day.

Obviously, the ability to create requires creativity. To produce creative work, certain characteristics such as aptitude, ability, interest, motivation, distinctiveness, personality traits, and exclusiveness all play a role.

Creative ability is different from the abilities of problem-solving, reasoning, intelligence, or even active thinking and thought processes. In historic anecdotes, it can often be appreciated that their creative ideas were inspired during a dream when they were not actively thinking of solving a problem.

An example of creativity can be seen in the real-life story of Archimedes of Syracuse. He had a problem that needed solving. King Hiero II provided a certain amount of pure gold to a goldsmith to make a crown fit for a king. King Hiero II was suspicious. Did the goldsmith use all the gold or was there foul play, and was the gold substituted by another metal? This problem required creativity from the great mathematician Archimedes, who did not want to damage the crown by melting it down. There was no way, during those times, to solve this riddle until Archimedes decided to take a bath. As he was climbing into the bath and was lying down, he noticed that his body mass displaced the water and the water level rose. The excited creative genius found the solution in a moment he least expected while not actively thinking or searching for it. He took to the streets. Naked! Shouting "Eureka!". The meaning of eureka is "I have found it!". Later, he successfully concluded that the goldsmith had added silver, not using all the gold provided by the king.

Archimedes' principle still stands thousands of years later. The volume of an object can be determined by measuring its displacement in water.

The great Sicilian excelled not only in math but also in physics, engineering, and astronomy. Up until his death at about age 75, he creatively invented. Hours of his life were devoted to discovering and solving problems.

What enabled Archimedes to create? What was required for him to successfully use his talents and fulfill the purpose of his life.

Creativity Illuminated

Archimedes required Earth to create! Without Mother Earth, in the form of silver and gold, a living body that has enough energy, and a brain with unique mental capacity, Archimedes would not have been the creative genius he was. This can be fully appreciated on his last day on Earth.

The death of Archimedes happened during the Second Punic War. General Marcus C Marcellus led Roman forces into the city of Syracuse in Sicily. Prior to that, after a two-year siege, the Roman forces were instructed to bring the great mathematician to meet the General. It was clear that Archimedes was well-known by that time. The Roman soldier approached Archimedes while he was focusing on a diagram, a mathematical diagram that needed solving. He declined the invitation to meet the Roman General, Marcellus, because he was busy and wanted to finish the problem and work. The Roman soldier became angry and struck a blow with his sword, the blow that took the life of Archimedes of Syracuse.

For us to live our passion creatively, we require a life-giving force. As Archimedes, we also need air in our lungs and blood pumping through our arteries, veins, and heart. We also require life in our bodies to be able to create. That mathematical diagram Archimedes worked on prior to his death had to be left behind.

For Archimedes to invent and practice his creativity in the fields of engineering, mathematic, physics, and astronomy, the creation had to be present. No creativity can be displayed without the creation, no physical problems to solve, no precious chemical elements such as gold found deep in the treasure trove of the Earth, no new discoveries such as gravity-defying aeroplanes to travel thousands of meters above the Earth cutting down travel time and saving hours.

Creativity normally follows phases, starting with the orientation phase. In this period, a problem is identified, which awakens curiosity, and the problem often presents itself as a question. After the initial orientation, the preparatory phase entails a collection of information from all available sources. It is during this phase where Archimedes studied various methods to analyze different metals. Children use this phase equally well by experimenting with moulds to make the perfect sandcastle or different colors to make the prettiest rainbow. The incubation phase is next. At this point in the creativity process, the potential creator hits a proverbial wall. All future attempts to solve and answer the question have failed or little ground has been made in finding a solution. The question, with all the information, is placed on hold temporarily. The timeframe can be anything from minutes to years. The problem is left unsolved. Unconsciously, the brain, in its immense capacity, never stops or forgets the problem. The person goes on with everyday life and does not focus on the problem at hand and may even forget about it, until the moment of illumination, the "ah-ha" moment. For Archimedes, that moment was when he ran naked through the street shouting "Eureka." Something seemingly insignificant triggered a thought and revealed the answer. Now all that is left to do is to test and evaluate if the solution solves the question or problem. It is possible that the answer appears immediately in a dream and no phases must be passed. However, some of these phases still apply. Have you experienced the phases of creativity? Well done! You have creatively made human existence better by doing so.

The Creation of God is documented in the Bible and even painted by Michelangelo in the fresco that adorns the ceiling of the Sistine Chapel in the Vatican in Rome. Michelangelo started this masterpiece in 1508 and finished it in 1512. The center panel of the fresco includes historic depictions of the separation of light and darkness, the separation of water and land, the creation of the sun, moon, and Earth, followed by the creation of Adam and Eve.

People flock to Rome to appreciate the fresco above their heads. Do we have the insight to see that even a masterpiece painted by a legendary artist requires inspiration from what already exists? If the creation did not exist, we would not be able to create; there would be no life.

We can truly take a lesson in creativity from the Creator!

Where did it all begin?

Let us start from the beginning. Not just your beginning, but the very beginning of Creation, according to a reference that provides an explanation for human existence.

My intention is to delve into the book of Genesis and history chapters written by humans who lived thousands of years ago. Information and insight was revealed to the writers of the Bible, from the Creator YAHWEH, who will be referred to as the Creator.

Disclaimer follows.

If you wish to continue reading, enjoy the journey "Creativity Illuminated." If this is not for you, I respect your decision and send you Love.

I overheard once that the Bible consists of love letters from the Creator to His beloved and faithful people. For this reason, the Bible is not for everybody and will not be appreciated by all. Imagine picking up a letter lying on the ground in a park. After picking it up and opening it, you realize that it is a letter proclaiming love to another. Will it have a deep impression on you? I believe that if this letter was written for you and signed off in the name of your beloved, it will touch your deepest core. In the same fashion, the Bible contains letters of love. The difference is the Creator of every human being – past, present, or future – cares and loves all His creations equally. It does not matter whether His creations accept Him or not.

Ecclesiastes 3:11

"He has made everything beautiful in its time. Also He has put eternity in their hearts, except that no one can find out the work that God does from beginning to end."

PART II

By delving into the creation in Part II, my hope is to connect you to the creative force of the ultimate Creator. Every day, by speaking words, the Creator established nature. Establishing the world far better than what we know it to be now, effortless yet powerfully created in only six days.

THE FIRST DAY CREATED

Genesis 1:1

"In the beginning God created the heavens and the earth."

Heavens and Earth were created. To know that the creation started with the distinction between heavens and Earth allows for a perspective evaluation. Heavens, in plural, refers to galaxies, and Earth is only one galaxy of a multitude of galaxies. The Milky Way is the galaxy in which Earth is created, very specifically mentioned in God's recollection of His creation. After mentioning the creation of heavens and Earth, the creation in other galaxies receive no further mention. However, the creation of Earth is elaborated on extensively. A possible reason for this is that the Creator knew how curious we as humans would be. Human beings have the intellect to be inquisitive about how Earth came about. He focused on how He created Earth, to make Earth habitable and sustain human life.

Genesis 1:2

"The earth was without form, and void; and darkness was on the face of the deep. And the spirit of God was hovering over the waters."

Day one of the Creation. This is the day when God's Love for the human race was demonstrated in action. You know how words from a loved one can mean very little when it is not followed by actions? Well, the deeds of God in making Earth habitable for human life preceded words. His spirit hovered over the waters, surveying how He can make the void of space into something new, a place that has never been. This is creativity in action.

Genesis 1:3-4

"Then God said, 'Let there be light'; and there was light. And God saw the light, that it was good; and God divided the light from the darkness."

What is the value of light? Naturally, the value of light can be appreciated while driving in a pitch-dark area. Instinctively, the driver must be more alert to avoid an accident. It can be a life or death situation, and fear is an emotion that is experienced in the absence of light.

I recall my very first mountain bike ride at night. It was a two-man-team race over three days with the first stage being a night ride. The organizers advised the participating riders to have strong headlights as well as a light on the handlebars of the bicycle. My friend assured me that she had extra lights and would bring them to the race for me to use. All sorted! We assembled the lights on my helmet and bicycle, and off we went. How much fun we had! We cycled effortlessly on the fast single tracks, as there was still enough daylight left before the sun shone its last rays. Through more single tracks, jeep tracks and forests we cycled, passing other woman teams; we were flying. It became increasingly darker and it was time to switch on the much needed lights.

The headlight on my helmet shone brightly, but the light on my handlebars was weak. Riding farther, it became increasingly difficult to see the road ahead. I had to ride on instinct, my fear levels rising. Then it happened! The headlight on my helmet went out and being the rider at the front, darkness fell over our two-woman team. I went over a bump and hit a rock. I went down hard, falling, to the right, off the bicycle. Ouch! My hip ached immediately as the rock hit a sensitive spot. However, I climbed back on my bicycle without too serious an injury to continue the ride. "Ride behind me" were the words of my friend.

The light on her helmet and bicycle made all the difference. That little bit of light instantly gave us more visibility to see the road ahead. The light aided my vision and guided me, and, following her lead, we reached the end of the stage.

Light also plays a vital role in our psychological state. Whether it is pain that keeps a person from sleeping, someone lost in the woods or having to spend the night in the darkness, a new day begins with the rising sun, bringing hope with it. Light fuels hope! Suddenly the eyes can see what was hidden in the darkness, dispelling fear and providing direction.

God knows the value of light and He provided an abundance of light for us. He even said that it was good. God Himself provided light, and He took the light and separated it from the darkness.

Genesis 1:5

"God called the light Day, and the darkness He called Night. So the evening and the morning were the first day."

"Opposites attract" is a phrase that is often used in relationships. This is usually between a couple that has met and get along well, but there will be some relationship challenges due to their opposite personality traits, religions, gender, political stances, to name but a few. When surveying how the creation was formed, opposites are rife. Let us consider the separation between light and darkness and, further, day and night. They are complete opposites.

Opposites can be appreciated in the creation of man. Adam and Eve, or male and female. Taking the opposite idea further to the interior aspects of man, the psychologist Jung talked about the "shadow." The shadow can be appreciated and simplified in my example of opposites to be the darker self. Jung voiced that, once he could appreciate and incorporate this darker shadow self into his personality, he made peace with himself, and this brought tremendous calmness to him. I can relate to the psychologist Jung's analogy to the shadow. I have also encountered this shadow; the small voice that is present throughout the day, often speaking opposites of good, always questioning motives. Two phrases continue to be the shadow's mottos. Who do you think you are for wanting to do or achieve that? You are not good enough! Amidst the continued racketing of the shadow, or what I have come to understand of it, is the dark one Satan. I have come to understand that the Triune God is good. Although we live in a time where the fight between good and bad, between light and darkness, seems to have escalated, we can simply stand as witnesses of the good and the light – the good and the light in nature, in our surroundings, and within ourselves and each other. The only way forward for me was to accept that I too am very capable of inflicting hurt and pain but that the intention of my doing so and how it is done will be a sufficient effort to try and not cause hurt and pain. If the intention is pure and good in being, doing, and serving, very few people, and even the darker side dare not point a finger your way. Let me take it a step further in saying that when you have acknowledged that you are capable of being dark but you choose the path of love, a beautiful revelation will be made to you. You will be surprised that, on the other side of your best efforts to love your neighbor as much as you have come to love yourself, you are looking into the eyes and heart of your Creator, and then your life's purpose will open the way for you and result in true happiness.

The concept of opposites applies equally to nature. Have you ever been in any natural disaster? Has a friend or family member related their story of a tsunami, hurricane, or natural hydrological disaster? It is during these times that the Creator is often blamed for taking life or causing destruction. It is my opinion that the Creator is good and remains good, even during natural disasters. In nature, opposites can be seen when watching the waves of the ocean. Throughout the day, the height and strength of the waves and currents change with the change of tides, which are attracted by the various cycles of the moon. This is made obvious by the use of low tide, where the waves are smaller, perfect swimming conditions, especially for younger children venturing into the ocean for the first time. Then high tide begins to creep in. Lifeguards send out a warning. The water level rises, the waves become bigger, and the currents under the surface of the water are strong enough to drag a person out to sea. Perfect example of opposites?

Imagine a peaceful day at the sea, bodies basking in the sun, beverages enjoyed, and sandcastles masterfully created. A glorious day on the beach! Then, we wake up on Boxing Day, 26 December 2004, and people are screaming. The news reports an earthquake off the West coast of Sumatra. There was a rupture along a fault line between the Indian Plate and the Burma Plate. Waves as high as 30 meters are seen and the resultant flooding caused 227,898 people to lose their lives. The city of Banda Aceh in Indonesia was the most affected area. The 2004 Boxing Day disaster is dubbed the deadliest natural disaster ever to be recorded in history. Earth vibrated about 1 centimeter and triggered other earthquakes, even as far up as Alaska. It caused a humanitarian response where people came together to support those affected. A donation exceeding 14 billion US dollars was made.

The Creator is good all the time, even to those people who have lost their lives and their families. When the creation demonstrates its opposite to what we have come to appreciate as an uneventful peaceful day on Mother Earth, then surely the opposite day can be accepted without judging the Creator of it. This realization caused me to encourage a thankful attitude daily for what we are gifted and to preserve those gifts. When you give a valuable gift away, you hope it will be appreciated, used wisely, and looked after by the recipient. This will surely make you happy, right? Especially if it was something you valued highly. However, you have relinquished any control over what the other person does with this valuable gift. Is it not similar in nature, where Mother Earth was gifted to us?

Earth has been created with resources in abundance. It is not simply one gift but a multitude of gifts that keep giving and increasing, the most precious gift ever given.

Do you think we have looked after the Earth since its creation?

THE SECOND DAY CREATED

Genesis 1:6-8

"Then God said, 'Let there be a firmament in the midst of the waters, and let it divide the waters from the waters.' Thus God made the firmament, and divided the waters which were under the firmament from the waters which were above the firmament; and it was so. And God called the firmament Heaven. So the evening and the morning were the second day."

Earth has been created by God for human life, with vast amounts of water on its surface, life-sustaining and life-giving. The need for water to sustain life can be seen in the percentage of water found inside our bodies. An average of 60% of the male's body and 50% of the female's body is made up of water. Water in the human body can be found in various areas, namely interstitial fluid, intracellular fluid, extracellular fluid, plasma in the blood, muscles, organs, and fatty tissues. The reason why I am going into a detailed description is to make you realize how important water is to sustaining life and to cultivate an appreciation of water in the Creation, and how much God made the Earth life-sustaining by dividing the waters under the firmament from the waters above the firmament.

Place your feet on the ground. Even if you are standing on grass or leaves, when you remove the ground cover from under your feet, you will encounter the hardness of the ground on which you are standing. The firmament amid the waters was created on the second day of the Creation. It is firm enough to divide the vast masses of water from each other on the horizontal plane and also firm enough to differentiate water on the vertical plane. When reading this verse in Genesis for the first time, it only now comes as a surprise that the firmament is called Heaven. Is the firmament not the ground and earth to which gravity so effortlessly holds us down? Or is Heaven as firm and sure as feet anchored on the ground?

Heaven, a place longed for and hoped for by many who suffer on Earth. Heaven is appreciated by many different religions, not only Christian. It is a place removed from Earth and, in a single word, Heaven, there is a surprising shared connotation which exists between opposing religions. The shared perception and belief is that Heaven is an enlightened place of peace, a place that humans can reach when they have proven themselves to be good and at peace with others. Heaven is seen as superior to anything experienced on Earth.

Who will go there? Is anybody there yet? The Creator or angels perhaps? In the Bible, a few had been fortunate enough to experience a glimpse into Heaven. Jesus, after His resurrection, ascended into Heaven and gave a promise to come back to Earth and fetch the faithful to the place prepared specifically for them. They would be awarded with an eternity with the Creator.

Criticism is often voiced when it comes to faithfulness and good deeds towards others to gain access to Heaven, a special place. The argument raised questions how sincere these good deeds really are if they are expected by the Creator to be granted access into Heaven. I agree!

In giving and doing good, the intention has to be true. A faithful disposition can, however, be maintained when, if the giver has a deep relationship with the Creator or wishes to strive to have a closer relationship, that person delves deep into the interior self. To have such a deep relationship with the Creator, intentions must be pure. It can then be proven that the good deeds performed towards others is in direct obedience of the Creator and also sacrificial of one's self. As Jesus epitomizes, the sacrificial call to obedience.

1 John 3:16-19

"By this we know love, because He laid down His life for us. And we also ought to lay down our lives for the brethren. But whoever has this world's goods, and sees his brother in need, and shuts up his heart from him, how does the love of God abide in him? My little children, let us not love in word or in tongue, but in deed and in truth. And by this we know that we are of the truth, and shall assure our hearts before Him."

Reaching your Heaven is a deeply personal experience. Once the fear of judgement by others comes into consciousness, then perhaps the conscience is speaking loudly. You should listen and investigate your intentions.

Is the conscience in the modern world in which we live still helpful, acting in truth? How much do we numb the warnings of our conscience when it comes to making decisions and resisting temptations?

Surely instant gratification plays a role because everything is so easy today, and this affects our behavior and decision making. Want a meal? Drive through a drive-thru at a fast-food outlet or go to a restaurant. Washing dishes has been made easy by loading the dishwasher. A five-million-dollar handshake secures the deal to tenders to a company rather than advertising the work externally. Who will say no to an easy deal and quick money? The conscience must be numbed to proceed. Good intentions have gone out of the window. Numbing is required to be able to wake up every morning and cover up any leads to avoid the shame on a family. Can you keep that secret forever? Let our hearts and conscience not condemn us!

To attain your Heaven, the instruction is to love in deed and truth, to say no to offers that violate your intentions. Knowing what you stand for will illuminate your intentions. Doing good deeds and love towards others will then be a sincere act. You should not be concerned about the opinion of others because you will be able to trust yourself.

Decisions will be made in truth, there will be no more shame, and perhaps there will be a walk of love.

1 John 3:20-22

"For if our heart condemns us, God is greater than our heart, and knows all things. Beloved, if our heart does not condemn us, we have confidence towards God. And whatever we ask we receive from Him, because we keep His commandments and do those things that are pleasing in His sight."

My intention is to write the words that God places in my spirit and heart. Remember Paul, Luke, Mark, Matthew, to name but a few writers of the Bible. This vision comes from a voice in my being to write about the Triune God and the promises made to Mankind, good and pure promises. Love from the Triune God is an action plan and not merely words in the Bible. With this vision in mind, I received this word recently.

John 15:4-6

"Abide in Me, and I in you. As the branch cannot bear fruit of itself, unless it abides in the vine, neither can you, unless you abide in Me. I am the vine, you are the branches. He who abides in Me, and I in him, bears much fruit; for without me you can do nothing."

LOVE CREATED: FLOW OF LOVE IN NATURE

Genesis 1:9-10

"Then God said, 'Let the waters under the heavens be gathered together into one place, and let the dry land appear'; and it was so. And God called the dry land Earth, and the gathering together of the waters He called Seas. And God saw that it was good."

The abundance of Yahweh can be appreciated in nature. In South Africa, water has become a scarce commodity. The dam levels have dropped in the Western Cape over the last number of years, and there has not been enough rain to fill them to supply the human needs. Adding to the concerning decrease in water is the vast number of South Africans and others moving to Cape Town and the surrounding suburbs. The beauty of the Western Cape district is unmatched. Beautiful, yet so harsh and, lately, thirsty. This region was named the Cape of Storm by Jan van Riebeeck when he landed on the Cape shores in 1698. The Theewaterskloof dam is the main source of water for Cape Town and the measured level at its lowest was 12.9%.

Water restrictions were implemented. Restriction levels were introduced by the governing authorities and named level-six restrictions. Fifty liters per household was all that was allowed.

Water was sent from all corners of South Africa, trucks full of water. The community involvement was heartwarming to see. Prayers were said, and tears were cried. Why was God allowing it? Was the Western Cape to become one big desert? Had we stripped nature to its core, causing weather changes because of human greed?

Then the heavens opened. It will take years to restore the water levels in the dams, some predicted. What did I tell you! When the Creator provides, He does so in abundance, so different from how we often give.

While writing to you, the water levels of the dams are at an average of 50%, from a low level of 21%. I recall a video taken of a cloud-break over a dam, one of the showers responsible for the restoration process of increasing the water levels in Cape Town. The cloud erupted over the dam like a shower being turned on at full pressure, not sparingly. The snow started falling shortly after the rain, with more blessings and bringing more hope for water when the snow melts.

A true winter rainfall was experienced in the Western Cape district and the overwhelming feeling of thankfulness to the Creator was felt. The feeling of how we are bogged down by human needs rings true in this true-life example of the water shortage. We may strive for more, according to the Maslow hierarchy of needs and levels of achieving. Once we lack on the level of a basic physiological need – for example, a lack of water to drink, wash, clean, or cook with – it is very difficult to strive to serve our neighbors by gifting water. It may also be more difficult to strengthen our spiritual relationship.

Love is like water.

Ice melts and water flows. It drips down a mountain into a stream. A stream may meet others like it and flows into larger streams, with the end destination being a river. Although specific rivers are close to the original mountain and streams, the stream can also flow and feed into new streams leading to other rivers. Nature does not hold back! It gives in abundance. A river in full flow receives the water given to it and then freely shares the water along its path. Rivers are not picky and do not remember the year of drought when that stream could not provide water. No exclusivity can be found in the flow of water. Streams willingly give water abundantly, perhaps because, in nature, the realization exists that the Creation is a gift that can only be shared. There is no razorlike focus on only one stream with an expectation of water to continue the flow of nature. The ultimate Provider and Creator will take care of the needs in nature.

The river looks ahead. It has a duty to keep flowing amidst distractions, rocks, and trees falling into its bed. It needs to find a new path. This is the river's focus. How does it flow? A river was created to flow. Flowing to serve mankind and sustain nature are the purposes of streams and rivers. They are life-giving.

Trying to restore lost momentum, when the river is faced with obstacles in its path, it pushes on, relentless in the pursuit of finding a new way to flow and to serve. To serve is the only purpose it knows. Instinctively the river knows; it has been created this way. Then, at last, a glimmer of hope amidst the obstacle in the way. A little bit of hope is all that is required. No sadness, no desperation. A new path presents itself, over or around an obstacle. Once momentum has been restored and new water has filled the river's belly, it keeps flowing. It doesn't look back to the obstacles, chastising them! The river rejoices because, at last, it is strong enough to flow, stronger because of the obstacles, perhaps even thanking them for the newly-found strength and resilience and knowledge to overcome such obstacles. Forgiving the temporary frustration of obstruction, lack of purpose, and inability to serve, the river does not look at obstacles the same way we as humans do. It looks back to thank the resourceful streams, mountains, and sources that provided the much-needed motivation to keep persisting amidst the difficulties. What happens next?

It flows! The flow of liquid from one point to another. The abundance of flow can be seen in nature around you, and as you are aware now, water flows inside you.

This is the beauty of the flow in nature. Perhaps appreciating the flow in nature and learning from it can help us to understand the Creator's love.

In nature, water takes on various forms. It is solid in the icy winters in the Alps, the rock-hard ice melting during season changes which allows for water to flow down mountains and into streams and rivers, into a network of multiple bends and turns, but the flow continues if there is enough water.

A river flowing in full flood has enormous strength in contrast to times when it gently flows over a rock or a root. Love can also be a force to be reckoned with. At times, we need to love our neighbors so hard when they are in turmoil. At other times, love needs to be gentle. To know love's flow and strength requires a close connection with the Creator, for we cannot always know the deepest feelings of our neighbor. There are times in life when we are struggling when feelings are difficult to convey to others. Words are few, yet much love is needed. Sadly, it is challenging to ask for support. For love to flow like a river, the close connection through the Holy Spirit helps us, guiding us and making us sensitive to the needs of others.

Water in the river doesn't have to be told what to do, order by another. The water does not ask permission to flow; it only knows how to flow. The water doesn't know how to do it another way. What happens down the river doesn't concern the current state of flow. It isn't flowing in anticipation of the waterfall waiting in the distance or the dam wall ready to stop its movement forcing it to remain and stopping its flow. Water obeys to commands of nature. It is not always easy to love...love cannot be concerned with the outcome.

Intensity of water flow varies when considering the amount of water, the pressure of the water, and the surface area in which the water flows. A gentle stream can be so subtle, yet, over a long period, the erosion of its flow is visible. It can smooth a rock into a rounded shape that can be appreciated with fingers or the palm of a hand through touch. Even moss and slimy sediments can be appreciated.

What does gentle flowing water do to you? How does it make you feel? Peaceful, calm, relaxed, happy, and thankful? Observing the flow of water in a river brings about tranquility to the observer. The observer does not have to have the ability to see the water; he/she can simply listen. The listener knows where he/she is – next to a river, a stream, or the ocean – by simply listening. There is no need for sight.

The force of water is unparalleled. A gentle stream can flow into a powerful river. In heavy rainstorms, the water's force can be so enormous that people get swept away in the water. Life gets lost.

A river in full flood is treacherous. No human can withstand its force. Its flow will move rocks and trees from their once secured position, and the momentum can be devastating to any bystanders observing the flow.

A tsunami is the perfect demonstration of the power of water.

Love can be compared to a tsunami. Love with the might of a tsunami has the highest highs and the lowest lows compared to when nature settles and the devastation is surveyed. To love your neighbor as you love yourself will also come at a price, similar to the price of the damage caused by a tsunami. The price that will have to be paid for the purest enduring form of love is an open heart. A heart forced open by enduring love, the kind that Jesus demonstrated while hanging on the cross, will be life-changing. This is my love journey.

THE THIRD DAY CREATED

Grass, herbs, and fruit trees were the focus of the Creator.

Genesis 1:11-13

"Then God said, 'Let the earth bring forth grass, the herb that yields seed, and the fruit tree that yields fruit according to its kind, whose seed is in itself, on the earth'; and it was so. And the earth brought forth grass, the herb that yields seed according to its kind, and the tree that yields fruit, whose seed is in itself according to its kind. And God saw that it was good. So the evening and the morning were the third day."

What power for the Creator to say, "let the Earth bring forth" with words He created!

It is the abundance in the creation that I want to pause at for a moment. When a product is made in a factory, there are set targets that need to be met. A hundred per hour or perhaps a thousand per hour. It is measurable. Productivity of employees is measured by how many items are produced per hour, per day, per month, or per year. Statistics are then used to compile performance sheets and generate visible graphs or charts. Graphs or charts are used in the performance assessment of the employees and the company. Salary increases and yearly bonuses are calculated by using these statistics of productivity.

The same company receives a letter asking for a donation of the product that will relieve the suffering of citizens in need. The counting continues. Fifty boxes can be donated; any more than that will leave a dent in sales and earnings. Losing money will not be accepted, but we have an abundant mentality, so we will help.

The Creator simply says, "let the Earth bring forth". He does not say that a thousand square meters of grass will be enough, that only ten different types of herbs will grow on Earth, or that two fruit trees in the Garden of Eden will be enough. No!

Everything created in nature is abundant. There is no scarcity. There is more than enough grass and plenty of herbs and fruit. Grass is classified as the Poaceae plant family. It is interesting to know that not only lawn grass falls under the plant family Poaceae, but so do natural grasslands, cereals, bamboo, and pastures. In the abundant nature of the Creator, 12,000 species and 780 different grass genera varieties can be found. Mother Earth was literally colored in with a wide variety of ground substances in the form of grasses which will abundantly provide for the need of every human being. The enormity of the third-day creation can be appreciated, where about 40% of land area is covered by grasslands, which include prairies and savannahs.

Grass was created to provide staple food for many nations in the form of cereal grains found in rice, barley, wheat, millet, maize, and forage grasses that feed animals and humans. Not only does the grass family fill our stomachs, but it allows us to have building materials such as thatch, straw, and bamboo to construct shelters and homes. Do you enjoy a cold beer? Then I am excited to tell you that the Creator in all His might even allowed for you to enjoy a cold beer by creating cereal grains. Cereal grains go through a process of soaking and drying. The process, called "malting," is where the grains germinate and enzymes are developed, which modifies the starches in the grains into different types of sugars. Enjoy that beer or whiskey responsibly; it is a gift from the Creator through the inspiration of a creative human.

Herbs are the leafy, green, aromatic plants that flavor and beautifully garnish our food. Herbs do not only allow us to experiment with culinary flavors but they have also played a medicinal role since prehistoric times. Traditional medicine was created on discovery of various plant herbs. Have you taken an aspirin lately? An aspirin is made from the active metabolite from salicylic acid, and its source is the bark of the willow tree. The creation of willow trees allowed for pain-relief and fever reduction. The abundant care of the Creator!

The creation of fruit trees yielding fruit, with its seeds, is abundance epitomized! The Creator gives a gift that keeps on giving. Fruit has sustained animals and humans for centuries. Even Adam and Eve were given a diet of fruit to nourish them. Let us consider an apple. When last have you had an apple to eat? Do you remember reaching the core after biting into the fleshy outer parts? That is where the black seeds can be found. The seeds are not another fruit's seeds! No, it is created with the potential to create itself over and over again for thousands of years. In the core of a single apple, more than four seeds can be found. It doesn't merely double itself but quadruples itself. That is abundant indeed! Moreover, it is self-sustaining.

Fruit is mostly self-sustainable because of the inherent potential to replicate itself. However, it does rely on its Creator for much needed water, animals to spread the seeds, and humans to prune the fruit trees to produce more and better-quality fruit.

THE FOURTH DAY CREATED

Genesis 1:14-19

"Then God said, 'Let there be lights in the firmament of the heavens to divide the day from the night; and let them be for signs and seasons, and for days and years; and let them be for lights in the firmament of the heavens to give light on the earth; and it was so. Then God made two great lights: the greater light to rule the day, and the lesser light to rule the night. He made the stars also. God set them in the firmament of the heavens to give light on the earth, and to rule over the day and over the night, and to divide the light from the darkness. And God saw that it was good. Go the evening and the morning was the fourth day."

The Creator illuminated the Earth with two powerful sources of energy. Firstly, the sun, the greater light to rule the day, and then the moon, the lesser light to rule the night.

The sun is a star and is to the center of the solar system. The fiery plasma sphere is the most crucial energy source to sustain life on Earth. The sun is by far the heaviest body in the solar system; its total weight constitutes 99% of the entire Solar System. It is not only heavy but it's also enormous. Its diameter of 1.39 million kilometers is 330,000 times the diameter of the Earth. What makes the sun so heavy? Hydrogen accounts for 73% and helium accounts for 25% of its mass. The Earth is, thankfully, well protected from the intense heat of the sun as the sun is 27,200 light-years away from the Milky Way. The sun converts tons of matter into energy of which we, and all of the creation, are the benefactors. Photosynthesis is a process where organisms and plants use life-giving energy from the sun.

Light energy is converted into chemical energy to fuel growth.

The lesser light ruling the night is the moon. The moon is the only natural satellite of the Earth that is permanent. This astronomical body orbits the Earth. It is a staggering 384,400 kilometers away from Earth, yet it illuminates our planet, particularly during full-moon. As the Earth rotates, so does the moon, in synchronicity with the gravitational pull towards the Earth, influencing the tides of the ocean.

The Creator illuminated the Earth with two magnificent energy sources. This illumination precedes every human endeavor. It allows for the illumination of minds, hearts, and spirit, daily, consistently. Is love perhaps the illuminating factor?

The illumination of the Creator's love opens. It opens my heart while I am searching for divine inspiration to be able to put inspirational thoughts into words. Surely this will leave me different? You different? The old ways of doing and loving will have to make way for the new. Discovering the truth behind the Creator's love is vast yet freeing and wonderful, and perhaps I will be able to, in spirit, touch the Creator of Love.

THE FIFTH DAY CREATED

There is immense power in words. Can you relate to the power of words? Perhaps you have uttered words in the past that you have had to apologize for. They may have been to a family member or a friend when you gave them a piece of your mind. You lost all the filters and the harmful words flowed effortlessly out of your mouth. Did you see how words can hurt others? It may have been visible on their faces.

I have hurt a dear friend in a similar way. Preceding the incident, I realized that the environment where I worked at that time influenced me negatively. Relentless work, challenging relationships with colleagues, and ultimately being exhausted. My friend told me, in love, that I have changed and that she does not know me anymore. It was a truth that I was not ready to hear. My harsh words, spoken in two minutes, caused pain. Shame rushed through my body and mind; I knew it was unfair. However, being so tired, I walked away. I gave no apology.

Words are powerful! A beautiful example of how words can be used to build and not to break can be found in the Creation. The Creator's words created! The words that were preconceived in His celestial being were spoken in a clear purpose. The Earth's Creator was well aware that the creational masterpiece would take six days. It is my belief that He started creating with that end-point in mind. The end goal was the creation of human beings on the sixth day! Every created thing had to sustain all living things, including us.

The Creator's thoughts were carefully orchestrated into words. He had only to speak the following words:

Genesis 1:20-23

"Then God said, 'Let the waters abound with an abundance of living creatures, and let birds fly above the earth across the face of the firmament of the heavens.' So God created great sea creatures and every living thing that moves, with which the waters abounded, according to their kind, and every winged bird according to its kind. And God saw that it was good. And God blessed them, saying, 'Be fruitful and multiply, and fill the waters in the seas, and let birds multiply on the earth.' So the evening and the morning were the fifth day."

On the fifth day, the waters were filled with aquatic life. To put the enormity of the Creation, by adding aquatic life to the oceans, into perspective, I want to remind you that the oceans include the Arctic, Atlantic, Indian, Southern (Antarctic), and Pacific oceans. The distance of these oceans together amounts to 361,000,000 km^2, with researchers' estimations concluded that only 5% of the oceans have been explored. It is so vast that billions of people, over thousands of years, could not reach the fullness of the oceans and all the aquatic species that have been created by the Creator. Only 230,000 aquatic species are known to human beings after the exploration of only 5% of the World Ocean. How many more species move and live in the oceans? Is it then possible that we only know 5% of the amount and intensity of the love that our Creator has for us?

The oceans are not only expansive, but they are also very deep. The average depth is 3,719 meters deep, with the deepest part located in the western Pacific Ocean in the Mariana Trench with a depth of 10,995 meters. The deepest journey in the Mariana Trench was first undertaken in 1875 by the crew on the HMS Challenger. The deepest part in the ocean since then was named Challenger Deep. Few people reach these depths in the ocean. Most of us enjoy the very shallow waves at the foot of beaches.

How deep is the love of the Creator for humans? Do we seek the depths of the love or are we only exploring a fraction of love's depth?

The deeper we delve into Godly love, the more we must give to ourselves and others. We will not be called Challenger Deep, but perhaps Flying Free.

Birds were created on the same day as the creatures of the waters. Flying animals were created to conquer gravity and soar. Some bird species find it easier to fly than others. The eagle soars; it will seldom be spotted on the ground. It knows its created purpose. Eagles use the invisible currents of the air. Once off the ground, the eagle flaps hard with strong muscles, creating a flow of air over the wings, forcing the eagle higher. In the high mountains, the eagles use the wind that collides with the hills to glide upward with the wind, reaching their nests effortlessly.

Knowing the currents and waves of the Creator's love may allow for the life that is longed for by many living conscious beings. The birds in the air, the creatures in the oceans, the crawling and walking animals in the creation know this way of life and being. They know the love of the Creator. Do you want to know this love?

Genesis 1:24-26

"Then God said, 'Let the earth bring forth the living creature according to its kind: cattle and creeping thing and beast of the earth, each according to its kind'; and it was so. And God made the beast of the earth according to its kind, cattle according to its kind, and everything that creeps on the earth according to its kind. And God saw that it was good. Then God said, 'Let Us make man in Our image, according to Our likeness; let them have dominion over the fish of the sea, over the bird of the air, and over the cattle, over all the earth and over every creeping thing that creeps on the earth.'"

In the creating, the Creator loved what was created by speaking words that were good, blessing the creation in the fifth and sixth days. Love was already spoken to all living things and beings from the onset. Creation, nature, and living beings were all created good and received a blessing. Perhaps the blessing can be compared to the artist ending the masterpiece by adding a signature. We all received a signature of love from the Creator.

PART III

Now, you may ask: but what about the creation of Adam, the first human? It is not a slip of memory. The Creator firstly established a habitable environment before making humans. The care in the provisions made shows a deep love.

Part III is separated to demonstrate the care and love with which we were created. Consistency shown in this kind of Godly love breaks all barriers and removes all obstacles in its path. No human mind can comprehend its depths and the enduring peace that flows out of the Creator's love. It cannot be earned by doing but merely appreciated by being and knowing the Source.

CREATION OF MAN

Genesis 1:27-31

"So God created man in His own image; in the image of God He created Him; male and female He created them. Then God blessed them, and God said to them, 'Be fruitful and multiply; fill the earth and subdue it; have dominion over the fish of the sea, over the birds of the air, and over every living thing that moves on the earth.' And God said, 'See, I have given you every herb that yields seed which is on the face of all the earth, and every tree whose fruit yields seed; to you it shall be for food. Also to every beast of the earth, to every bird of the air, and to everything that creeps on the earth, in which there is life, I have given every green herb for food'; and it was so.' Then God saw everything that He had made, and indeed it was very good. So the evening and the morning were the sixth day."

Human beings are created in God's image. Being created in the image of the God of love brings about the realization that love is part of our being. To comprehend this realization is personally difficult for me. Love is abstract. Where can the source of the Creator's love be found in our bodies?

Do the following activity with me! Take your right hand and lift it up. Lift up your hand to the level just below the eyes. Now look at your hand while you point with an index finger, similar to the way you will point a finger at somebody standing in front of you. Now turn the finger towards yourself. Where is your index finger pointing to?

The index finger points in the direction of the heart! The heart is often seen as the source of love.

THE HEART

To love is either instinctive when you're young or a deep understanding of your own humanity when you become an adult. It is surely not a superficial experience, or is it? Love songs come to mind. "Hit me Baby one more time, my loneliness is killings me and I must confess I still believe…," "I can't live when living is without you". I must confess, I enjoy a good beat in a song, and especially a good love song. Does our generation believe that this is what love is about?

Social media has become a part of our lives, where we share our deep personal lives with people outside of family and friends. This brings about a new dimension to interacting in relationships. Sharing engagements and weddings have become favorite moments on social platforms. At times, pictures show the newly engaged couple on their phones rather than in each other's arms.

Are we diluting love? The love of the Creator is deep, and this can be seen in how wonderfully the source of love – the heart – has been sculpted. The human heart that beats in your own chest has been sculpted in an anatomically and physiologically interacting fashion, unlike any motor that has ever been made by human hands.

The human heart is without a doubt the most genius self-sustaining motor ever created. It has the capacity to help sustain life for over a hundred years. Without maintenance or charging required, it beats relentlessly. This enduring muscle pumps life-giving blood to the rest of the body. Deoxygenated blood moves to the heart while oxygen-rich blood moves away to feed the body at a cellular level. Studying the intricacies of the heart can provide a glimpse into the love of its Creator.

Creativity Illuminated

As the heart beats, so the love of the Creator is present for all human beings. This love is not subjected to mood, time of the day, or what we do right or wrong. It is as enduring and steadfast as the beat of the heart.

To feel how the heart beats, place your hand on top of your chest. Do you know where your heart sits? The heart sits securely and snugly in the thoracic cavity and is protected by the thoracic wall. The thoracic wall is made up of ribs and the sternum bone in front of the chest and the spine at the back. Vital organs are placed in this thoracic cavity. The lungs and the heart are well protected to sustain life.

Now move your hand in between in the middle of the chest bone (sternum) where the line drawn between the nipples meet. For males this is quite accurate whereas for female this line can vary. Good, you found it! Lastly, shift a few centimeters to the left. You are now touching your own heart. Close your eyes and feel what happens under your hand. Breathe in slowly through the nose and out through the mouth. Relax completely and just feel.

Do you feel how strong your heart beats? Sit back and allow your heart to beat under your hand. It beats to its purpose for which you were created by the Creator. "When you are born, your purpose was placed in your heart," as Kahlil Gibran said. Trust the love of the Creator as much as you trust the heartbeat in your chest.

The heart, a muscular organ, is surrounded by fibrous layers. The first fibrous layer which protects the heart is called the pericardium. It is a sac-like structure on the outermost surface. Another layer, the epicardium on the inside, is fixed to the heart. These two layers are separated by a very narrow space filled with fluid. The fluid acts as a lubricant as the heart beats in the sac.

We are also surrounded by two layers of protection. The Creator surrounds every human with a layer of love and a layer of grace. The layer of love gives you the courage to wake up daily and pursue a purpose or a task, to work to provide for your children and to create that masterpiece or chase your dreams. Love provides the courage to continue in all of these endeavors, not just one. To attain this courage in love, one thing is needed. You must know the love, feel the love, experience the love, and grow in the love of the Creator.

The layer of grace surrounding us daily is the protection from harm, the sunrise in the morning, the rain falling from the sky, the child you held in your arms after the birth that went well, the friend you met at the rugby game, the friend who became a best friend, the lady who became your wife, the man who became the father of your children. This is the grace of the Creator.

The grace and love we have from our own Creator can be compared to the muscle that beats in our chest, our heart.

There is a muscular organ called the myocardium, which consists of cardiac muscle cells. The inside of the muscle, delving deeper into the heart, reveals a thin layer of endothelial cells. These endothelium lines are the chambers and interior of the heart's blood vessels.

It is not only important to know that the Creator's love and grace surrounds us, but it is crucial to be aware that we have to actively work on our interior life. As the heart is lined on the inside with endothelial cells, we need to also mature our inner thoughts which when controlled, allow us to move closer to this love.

The heart has a left side and a right side, each performing its own function. Furthermore, the heart is also divided into a top, which hosts the atria, and a bottom, where the ventricles are housed. The atria are chambers through which blood flows from the veins to the ventricles. Contraction of the atria allow blood to flow. Blood flows and fills the ventricles. Atrium contraction aids the movement and filling of the ventricles. However, it is found to not be essential for filling. Take a look at how a passive system allows the blood to move through the heart.

Contraction can be compared to our efforts to love the Creator, which will attract much peace. However, even if there is no effort made, the love of the Creator will still flow. Love always flows towards us like the blood that moves from the atrium to ventricle to provide life-giving blood to the body.

Between the atria and ventricles on both left and right sides of the heart, atrioventricular valves are situated, allowing the movement of blood from atria to ventricles. No flow exists from ventricles to atria, the bottom of the heart to the top of the heart. Names are given to the atrioventricular valves: the right called the tricuspid valve and the left called the bicuspid valve or mitral valve. A passive flow exists through these valves due to the pressure differences across the atria and ventricles and the valve itself.

Pressure differences help the flow of blood. Once the pressure exceeds that of the ventricle, the valve is pushed open. When the same ventricle that received the blood reaches its capacity, the valve between them closes. No blood should flow back to the atrium but rather into the pulmonary trunk on the right sides of the heart and back into the aorta on the left ventricle's side.

The beauty of anatomy and physiology can be appreciated in deeper reflexion of these atrioventricular valves. When the interior work has been done, changing thoughts, thinking in stillness, thinking about the grace and love of the Creator, finding quiet moments in the day and feeling the powerful beat of the heart under your hand, then love will passively fill you. By attracting this love into your life so abundantly and filling it to capacity, the only possible result is to overflow with love. Love will spill out and flow to a neighbor, spouse, child, or colleague. A love so pure and true, from a source so abundant, cannot be contained in a vessel. It will passively and effortlessly move.

Although love has the ability to passively move, effort is valuable in sustaining good relationships. It can be appreciated how a heart that had to beat fast during exercise becomes stronger and healthier as the body become increasingly fitter. Likewise, a relationship will be stronger and healthier with more effort from both parties.

In the heart, blood moves through these valves, and papillary muscles keep the valves from pushing up towards the atria. Fibrous supporting structures called chordae tendinea support the papillary muscles. The chordae tendinea stop the papillary muscles from everting, ensuring the blood keeps moving in the correct direction.

The Creation on the sixth day blows my mind! Not only did the Creator make all beasts and animals, but He created man so intricately that fibrous structures support the papillary muscles in the valves, ensuring the heart will not collapse in on itself. We are wonderfully created!

Two more valves control flow from the ventricles into the pulmonary artery and aorta, called the pulmonary valve and aortic valve respectively. These valves have a half-moon shape. The half-moon shape gives the valves their name, semilunar valves. The flow is controlled passively again due to pressure differences.

A half-moon-shaped valve between the bottom half of the heart (ventricles) controls the flow of blood to the lungs and the rest of the body. A moon-shaped valve is created to illuminate the night, as on the fourth day of the Creation. Love, once it starts flowing past the barriers which previously stopped its flow, will leave a trail of illumination. The illumination trail that will be carved out from that moment on will enlighten darkness like the moon sheds light on a dark night.

Ventricular contractions push the life-giving blood through the pulmonary and aorta and further into the systematic vascular system. This occurs with every heartbeat and the cycle starts over again.

A human vascular system is a distribution system that is cleverly created for physiological efficiency. Its main function is to deliver oxygen and nutrients to organs, muscles, ligaments, tendons, the central nervous system, endocrine system, skeletal system, and skin (organ).

The heart's main function is to transport blood between the lungs and body. It is a vital function because it clears the blood of any impurities and fills the blood in the lungs with oxygen which fuels and provides nutrients to the rest of body structures. Without blood, the systems of the body will cease working, cells will die, and the brain will stop. A brain without oxygen and rich blood will only last for a few minutes. The body is dependent on this life-giving blood and nutrients, just as we as humans are dependent on love. In the absence of a mother's love, a baby develops slower and no thriving can be seen. This remains true in adulthood where the need to show love and be loved remains until the last days. The naysayers will comment by saying they don't need love; an absence of love plays itself out daily. Loneliness is clear when a couple has been married for 40 years and then one of them passes away. It has often been seen that the remaining spouse passes away soon after.

The vascular system, the transport system of blood from the heart to the rest of the body and organs, comprises of arteries, arterioles, capillaries, venules, and veins. Let me explain each part separately.

Arteries act as pressure containers when the ventricle of the heart relaxes and the arteries receive the blood from the ventricle. Arteries have very little resistance to the flow of blood. Blood from the arteries move to the next transport system called the arterioles. Arterioles offer some resistance to flow and aid in arterial blood pressure regulation. From the arterioles, the blood is transported to its destination with the help of capillaries. Capillaries are the delivery men in the body. At the areas where capillaries are present, an exchange process occurs between the blood and the tissues that are in need of the nutrients contained in the blood. At the capillary level, exchange takes place. The exchange process is imperative to ensure the survival of the body. The waste products from the tissues are deposited back into the capillaries and the capillaries provide much-needed oxygen-rich blood to the tissues.

The exchange process that occurs in the vascular system at the capillary level reminds me of the exchange process in relationships. Coveted friendships are characterized by this exchange process. It is a partnership where both parties understand that building a strong friendship bond requires effort. The effort that builds strong lasting friendship needs effort, time, and the Creator.

However, even in the strongest relationships, times can get rough when one person goes through difficult personal challenges. This is when love can act as a cleansing agent. The exchange process might not be equal. This is where the flowing of love from a spouse, family member, or friend has the ability to heal and assist. It is important to remain close to them and allow the love to flow.

There is no separation between the components of the vascular system and the continuous flow. The interdependence in the vascular system is present to fulfill the purpose of keeping the body healthy.

After the exchange occurs between the capillary and the arteriole level, the blood is now filled with waste products. The venules continue with the exchange process of fluids, metabolic waste products, and nutrients. The veins are responsible to take the deoxygenated blood, which is filled with waste products, back to the heart. The larger veins are responsible for taking the blood back to the heart, and the veins have a low resistance to the flow of blood.

Blood! Did you know that the average adult has between 4.4 and 5.5 liters of blood circulating in their bodies? Blood flows inseparably through the chambers of the heart, veins, and arteries in the lungs and throughout the body. Blood consists of cells and plasma.

Flowing love is not superficial but, rather, a deeper exchange of thoughts, moments in one's past, sharing of dreams and hopes, and thankfulness for the life gifted by the Creator. This mutual sharing allows healing, much like the cleaning that occurs in the blood at the tissue level.

It is in the plasma fluid of blood that the cleansing occurs. This liquid part contains ions, waste products, and gasses. The exchange occurs between the interstitial fluid in the capillaries and the blood that flows through it.

Love, through its flowing, is a cleaning agent, an energy generator, when the source of the love is from its Creator. It will bring fun and laughter into lives. Love never stops giving when it is rooted in its true purpose. The purpose of love is to serve others.

Erythrocytes, leukocytes, and platelets make up the cells that can be found in blood. Erythrocytes, at their main function, exhibit gas transportation. Leukocytes aid the immune system in fending off intruders that want to break down our immunity. Platelets play an important role in the clotting of blood.

As in the inside, so it is on the outside. Love, like leukocytes, can protect the couple from the harsh reality of life and hurt. Think back to a courageous act that, once envisioned, was taken by the horn. You did it! Amidst fear. Was there a loved one who pushed you or motivated you to do it? All we need to be brave and courageous is another person who loves and supports us, knowing that, when we fall, the person will be there to stretch out a hand, pick us up, and put their arms around us.

In loving, no real purpose exists except to serve.

EGO IN LOVE

Love, at its core, simply exists to serve. In this love, there is no place for the ego.

The ego, at its core, aligns all conscious thoughts on the self. An egoistic-driven person makes decisions that are self-directed, with or without feelings of exaggerated self-importance. It is an inward vantage point. What is in it for me? How can it benefit me?

Clearly, to love involves another motivation that informs conscious actions and motivation. Unlike ego, love is focused outward and onto others. How can I get to know and love that person better? How can I spoil my friend on her birthday?

Love is a force so strong and pure that the ego cannot stand up to it. It cannot be measured, or can it?

1 Samuel 13:14

"But now thy kingdom shall not continue: the Lord hath sought him a man after his own heart, and the Lord hath commanded him to be captain over his people, because thou hast not kept that which the Lord commanded thee."

The Creator, God, made a comparison between David and Saul. The tool used in the measurement is the quality of the heart. The Creator was looking for a man to lead His people and the measurement was made, and He found David's heart to match His heart the closest.

An adult's heart is approximately the size of the fist when fingers and thumb are rolled inside the palm. In length, the heart is 12 centimeters long, 8 centimeters wide, and 6 centimeters thick.

When the Creator sought a leader, he did not measure David's heart in centimeters. It was a deeper quality in the heart that informed His decision to choose David above Saul to be the captain of the ship, leader of the chosen people. Allow me to explain.

The Creator's selection criteria went much deeper. The chosen leader's heart had to be like the heart of the Creator; the personal ego must be suppressed. The heart that is uniform to the heart of the Creator will not only think of others more than of self but will also want to serve others with love. The heart that think about self or the own ego less and more about others leads me to conclude that the heart is not present in the brain.

The neural pathway in the human body is fascinating. A neural pathway is when a message is registered and transported to the brain and then acted on. Do you remember removing your hand from a hot stove? The neural pathway sends the message, in that split second, to the central nervous system to make the decision to remove the hand from danger. Allow me to compare this to a busy four-lane highway. Two lanes are designed to enter a busy city. One of the lanes entering the city is named the anterolateral or spinothalamic pathway. The vehicles moving on this pathway are plain and transport messages of "temperature", which can be compared to a red motor vehicle. There are a few fueling stations on the way into the city. The first transition is in the spinal cord; this is called the grey matter. After a very quick pit stop, it continues upwards through the anterolateral column of the spinal cord, destined for the next stop at the thalamus. In the thalamus, the vehicle connects with other vehicles on cortically projecting neuron motors. Almost at its destination, the thalamus projections are sent onwards to the somatosensory cortex, the brain. An interesting fact is that the most sensitive and most innervated areas of the human body are represented in this somatosensory cortex with larger areas. The lips, thumb, and fingers enjoy a larger area or hangout place in the brain than the leg or elbow, for example.

But the heart is not represented in the brain! Subdue the ego by not centering all thoughts on itself but consider a deeper way of being and doing. Love another human being as you love yourself. This characteristic is similar to the heart of the Creator.

The Creator measures the quality of a heart to the flowing in and out and giving to others.

The heart's outpouring of blood gives life. It nourishes the life-giving breath, providing oxygen to the lungs. It also nourishes your central nervous system. The thinking, decision-making, intuitive, voluntary, and involuntary demand-centers! Without the flow of blood from the heart, carrying oxygen to your brain, life will end.

The outward flow of what is in the heart is measured by daily practices and what a person talks about. The spoken words to others, through love, can uplift, nourish, and provide oxygen to the lives of others.

BREATH OF LIFE

The human brain, without oxygen, will shut down within six minutes. Oxygen is a necessity for human beings to stay alive and it starts in the oxygenation process in the lungs. It all started with the breath of the Creator. Even before the heart gave a beat, Adam received life, through the breath of the Creator, into lungs through the nostrils.

Genesis 2:7

"And the LORD God formed man of the dust of the ground, and breathed into his nostrils the breath of life; and man became a living being."

Man was not only created in the likeness of God but also received his breath into human lungs, allowing the first ever heartbeat to awaken. The moment the Creator breathed into Adam's lungs and awakened his heart is perhaps the Creation of love. The connection between the lungs and heart can provide more evidence to the interconnectedness between us, God, and Love.

Every heartbeat transports blood to the lungs. Deoxygenated blood must go through the lungs for oxygen to be added to the blood before the blood returns to the heart. Oxygenated blood is then transported to the rest of the upper and lower parts of the body.

Breathing oxygen in from the air around us enables the lungs to provide this valuable life-giving commodity.

A close connection between the heart and lungs is vital. The heart cannot decide to exclude the lungs from its existence like we often do with each other in relationships. A human is dependent on oxygen and a few minutes without this vital gas have dire consequences, such as death. As the heart and lungs are intrinsically connected for the length of our time on Earth, so is the connection between God and us. The Creator's breath ignited human existence, allowing inventions, creativity, relationships and, ultimately, love. To experience a life filled with love and service, interconnectedness with the Creator should be present and as close as the lungs and heart.

A connection with our Creator should not only be present but the desire of God is that this connection should be as strong as a mountain, an ox, or a lion. Is an ox or a lion strong on the day of its birth? Surely not! But it has the potential to be strong. A comparison is made between the strongest of animals and our connection with God. At times, building this connection is a slow process. It is important to understand that it is not God that is slow to love us. You know that longing you feel at times? How you miss someone? That is the gentle nudge of the Creator that He wants you to be closer. The Creator wants to have a closer connection with you.

For love to emanate out of us, we should have a strong connection with the Creator.

John 34:14-15

"If He should set His heart on it, if He should gather to Himself His Spirit and His breath, all flesh would perish together, and man would return to dust."

Have you noticed that you are made of flesh? Do you remember the first time you were introduced to the concept of pain? Our flesh is so easily injured. This is what is referred to when God uttered those words. The spirit and breath that ignited life into the first human is in fact a piece of the Creator. The flesh that you are able to feel with your hands is sustained by the Creator. It can be injured many times in a single day but an abundance of mercy and protection keeps us safe, whereas, in the historical biblical times, the

Creator destroyed human existence during Noah's time out of anger and disappointment. Only Noah, his family, and two of each animal species were saved. So much love has been bestowed by the Creator that even in sin we have not experienced the biblical time of Noah. The Creator needs to be revered for this mercy.

Job 33:4

"The Spirit of God has made me, and the breath of the Almighty gives me life."

A closer look at how the heart and lungs work in unison demonstrates the intricacy of the Creation of Man. On the interior of the body, organs are placed.

The circulatory system involves flow. The superior vena cava and inferior vena cava drains deoxygenated blood from the top and bottom part of the body into the right atrium. Blood containing waste products gets pumped from the body by the superior and inferior vena cava. The blood flows from the right atrium through the tricuspid valve into the right ventricle. From the right ventricle, the blood gets transferred to the lungs through the pulmonary vein.

After oxygenation in the lungs, the blood flows through the pulmonary arteries back to the heart. The pulmonary arteries drain in the left atrium where, through the mitral valve, it moves into the left ventricle. The aorta is responsible for pumping the oxygen rich blood from the left ventricle to nourish and feed the rest of the body for its survival.

A heartbeat is dependent on the SA node as an electrical notification to initiate the heart as a pump. The heart is intrinsically connected to the lungs in an exchange process. The shared responsibility of the connectedness between the lungs and the heart lies in achieving the goal of oxygenating the entire human body. This teamwork is so effortless and efficient, without an external manager telling them to work, motivating the heart to keep on pumping, and asking the lungs to reach the deadlines agreed upon. This is all achieved through the electrical message of a node that works automatically. When the Creator creates, it is in abundance and the fruit lasts.

It was, however, my heartbeat that was compromised at a young age.

HEARTBEAT

It is this heartbeat that has fascinated me from a young age. I was still a young girl, around 6 years old when I was asked by a total stranger to accompany him to a deserted field. Being very ignorant, I agreed. He kissed me, reassured me, and subsequently tried to rape me. The idea of sexuality was strange to me at that tender age, so I resisted and said no. Thinking back to that day, I wonder why he listened to me and stopped. He locked me in this little shack and I felt fear, the kind I never knew existed. It was at that moment my heart stopped beating, figuratively.

I was experiencing an unexpected terror and wanted, with every fiber of my being, to escape. I wanted to run as fast as I could to get back home, back to safety. That is exactly what happened. I escaped! My ignorance shattered. A young mind, not yet able to fully understand things, filled with terror. I ran home.

Looking back at my childhood years since that incident, I can honestly say that it affected me on many levels. One of the levels affected was my trust in men, my concentration in school and university, not being able to read with thought or comprehension, and a struggle with the Creator and my faith. A young mind with many questions. Why me? I believed that it was my mistake and this may have been the reason I didn't share this with my parents. It was the change in my heartbeat that I remember clearly. Since that traumatic moment, my heartbeat was faster and the rhythm somehow different, never settling or relaxed.

A heartbeat is consistent! The heart rate, however, changes. In an anxious situation, the heart rate increases automatically, fueled by the release of a hormone called adrenaline. You don't decide at that moment that your heart rate should increase in order to pump extra blood through veins and arteries. When adrenaline starts rushing through the body, the vital organs and muscles receive more blood at a faster rate. This enables the fight-or-flight response to the stressor. Run from trouble, as far and quickly as possible. The faster you run, the faster the heart beats blood to enable the muscles to function.

A heartbeat, on average, beats 80 times a minute. In a fit person, the beat can be as slow as 40 beats per minute. In the instance of fear or trauma, the heartbeat races up to over 150 beats per minute.

A constant rush of adrenaline coursed my body, making my heart beat faster, and, at one point, I even thought I had had a heart attack. My heart was broken.

The healing, although taking many years, started in silence, never telling about the shame because I agreed to it, right? Wrong! It is never okay to abuse in any way. Never! From that day, my heartbeat never regained its normal 80 beats per minute. It beats erratically, too fast, never normal.

I believe that the Creator provided a dose of extra love daily, which sustained me. Faithful, loving parents, heavenly and earthly, cared for me and, later, a loving husband. Sharing the trauma with Paul was the ultimate catalyst. He has helped me believe in love again.

The ordeal has made me different, strangely fiercer, more believing in the goodness of the Creator and His enduring love, and now I am writing this to you, feeling strangely at ease after my figurative heart attack.

A HEART ATTACK

The heart's flow is continuous and only stops when disease has sets in. Disease can cause a blockage in the heart with a lack of blood-flow through an artery or vein. Disease may even lead to a heart attack.

Can you imagine how a heart attack feels? Some among us have been through a heart attack and survived. Heart attack survivors, when speaking about their ordeal, often tell about the shock, fear, and pain. However, no living person can relate to how it must feel when a heart gives its last beat and stops. This machine, above all, was created to sustain life for years.

A different kind of blockage can also be present: the blockage to love. The ability to give and receive love is instilled from early childhood years. A person grows up with one of two underlying threads in a household: either to fear or to love. The underlying threads, teaching young children about fear and love, can be found in the environment, household, and community they are growing up in. Fear or love, both powerful teachers, affects a child's self-esteem and eventual character. Why is character important when talking about love? Love and character go hand-in-hand because of a deep sense of worth that is hidden in a person who grows up with fear. I can relate to fear and know how it affects the young mind of a child. Interestingly, I grew up in a loving home. My household environment taught me love and acceptance. However, an unsafe community allowed fear to creep in, affecting my character and ability to love. It took me 38 years to begin to understand and make sense of love and its power.

Love is like the heart that beats nonstop. Love provides nourishment and sustains life. To think that you don't need love to survive can be compared to a heart that stops beating. Similar to a heart attack, you will have to make a few trips to the emergency room and maybe even require surgery to repair the damage caused by a lack of love. You will experience moments where intense intervention will be required to continue to live a fulfilled and valuable life. A defibrillator can be applied to provide a shock to encourage the heart to beat again. The defibrillators in life can be felt in life events like the passing of a loved one, a lost relationship, or a miscarriage of a child. Alcohol, drugs, sexuality, and electronic devices can all, when used in excess, start to fill the void caused by a lack of love and healthy intimacy in relationships. The sustaining power of these numbing agents is only temporary and have no depth or longstanding happiness. A healthier longstanding medicine will make a positive change, growing to understand the flow of the Creator's love even when a blockage is present.

PART IV

The distance covered by this love created by the Creator further exceeds human understanding. It will not stop flowing in and around you, even when a blockage is present. The realization of how we fit into the creation, the bigger picture, and how much we are loved requires stillness beyond the rush around us. It requires humbleness compared to the ego and self-proclamation. It asks for nothing but gives everything.

CREATION OF LOVE: FLOW AFFECTED

The key question remains: how can we develop the ability to love, develop and sustain deep healthy intimate relationships, and experience joy?

Remember the flow of water in the river example given earlier, where the river encounters obstacles in its way and its flow is halted. In the dry season, the flow is already compromised and its flow is easily affected. The river may even stop flowing.

When our flow of love is affected because of disappointment or shame, it can be compared to this river in a dry season. The shameful experience I had to go through as a young girl affected love's flow in my life. It was difficult to receive love from the Creator and equally as difficult to give love.

Temporarily stopping the receiving/giving flow of love is not a problem while healing takes place. However, not healing from the hurt and growing in love is an enormous problem! Love is a strong healing power from the Creator. I experienced this healing power of love in my life and want to share it with you.

Let me tell you a secret. I haven't arrived yet. It requires a daily relentless closeness to the Creator and a walk in love to overcome obstacles and my past perceived failures.

In the face of obstacles and perceived failure, how can we bulletproof our interior landscapes? John C Maxwell gives seven abilities required to fail forward in his book 'The 8 Pillars of Excellence'[1], and I want to elaborate on these seven points to help you overcome and move forward in love.

1. Reject rejection

Rejection, at most times, involves another person. It is often seen that a rainstorm causes a deep sense of rejection; perhaps the bride feels that the Creator is ruining her perfect day with a rainstorm.

Rejection is a refusal, dismissal, or nonacceptance of a proposal. A rejection can be in business or relationships. Once a marriage or business proposal has been rejected, the body's physiological system and psychological system is triggered. This is where the tipping point lies in our reaction towards the perceived rejection. This tipping-point moment, if understood, holds the power to create positive change in how rejection is perceived.

Once your heart starts beating faster, beads of sweat starts lining your brow and a rush of heat through your body is accompanied by thoughts. Thoughts like "who do you think you are?" or "why did I even try?". Don't take the rejection personally! As soon as feelings of worthlessness enter your thoughts, that is when you have the most power to move forward. If you can take anything out of the criticism that will be helpful in improving your proposal, you can learn from it and grow towards your next proposal. Do not make it personal but rather affirm the positives. The fact that you worked relentlessly on the proposal is a positive. You displayed courage by approaching the girl of your dreams, asking your loved one to marry you, or closing the business deal. Affirm your efforts!

Don't get bogged down and allow the rejection to stop your next attempt.

2. See failure as temporary and know the sun will rise on your face

With a new day comes a new experience. Trust the process of becoming a truer version of yourself and a being that moves towards loving more. The rising of the sun in Africa is so consistent that, even in the colder winter months between June and August, the sun's rays provide a powerful serotonin release. So should a new day give hope, to know that a failure is temporary.

In the instance where your failure hurt others deeply and perhaps even caused loss, a deep need for help exists that is beyond the scope and vision of the book. Realizing pathological behavior can cause conviction and jail time, and in this instance, I am not referring to failures in this sense.

Hope should always be a part of every being, especially when you see a new day and have life and breath in you to change the course of your life.

3. See failures as isolated incidents and not lifelong disappointments

A mistake was made; you are not a mistake. It is easy to make this incorrect assumption by speaking negatively about yourself. The probability of the failure being an isolated incident is big. The sadness of an isolated incident of failure seen as a personal failure is that it can hold you back and becomes a lifelong disappointment.

4. Keep expectations realistic and intentions pure

After a failure or rejection, it will help to have realistic expectations or adapt your expectations according to the response. The girl or man of your dreams may have said no to a date but still wants to be friends with you – treasure the friendship by adjusting your expectations. Don't throw away a good friendship.

5. Focus on strengths

Strengths are those qualities, skills, or abilities unique to each person. For some, these strengths are clear from a very young age. Think of that musical virtuoso who starts playing that musical instrument and displays a clear talent. For others, me included, it may take 30 years to find these strengths. Think about Colonel Sanders, the Kentucky Fried Chicken founder. It took him many years and different occupations, including a steam-engine stoker, petrol station worker, and insurance salesman, before creating his secret recipe. He had suffered loss and only when he was at his wits end did he decided to make a last attempt at what he was good at. His last attempt to make something of his life was frying chicken. KFC is enjoyed by millions across the globe and his last attempt to focus on his strengths paid off! His legend outlasted him.

Is it possible to discover your strength before retirement? It will certainly help and will bring tremendous satisfaction and joy to be able to see the fruits of your labour.

Do you know what your area of strength is? Perhaps you have more than one? That is great! Now ask yourself this question: were you acting in your area of strength or your area of weakness when you experienced the failure?

Answering this question will give you direction and help your future progress. If you can honestly say that you were not busy in your area of strength, then you have two choices. The first choice is to put all your efforts into developing that area of perceived weakness; the second choice involves focusing on your area of strength.

When choosing to develop and improve the area you are weak in, much time and energy will be spent, but this can pay off. You can improve your area of weakness by reading, attending conferences, workshops, enrolling in courses, spending time with an expert in that field, and asking questions. Improving on your weaknesses can be a worthwhile investment and a wonderful adventure. It can open work opportunities in that field, and you may even become an expert and teacher.

Focusing on improving a weakness is for you if you have a patient attitude. A thick skin and a motto of "never give up" is helpful because of the past and future rejection you will have to endure.

When choosing to focus on improving on the area you know you are strongest in; this will also pay off and, I believe, will allow you to evolve and become a master of your field or craft. Working to improve an area of strength is equally as hard but will yield fruit faster and perhaps in more abundance compared to spending much time on improving a weak area. You will become an expert in that field after hard work and focus are applied. This is also encouraged by authors such as John Maxwell and Marcus Buckingham.

Personally, I had to work hard on personal weak areas from a young age. This has helped me to discover my strengths, which I am still trying to fully understand. An area of strength is a concept that eluded me for most of my 38 years and sound like an act in a drama movie. I had great difficulty reading and concentrating. I had to work hard for every mark, hours at a time. It felt like I was walking in a clay-mire. Moving slowly but moving forward!

This reminds me of the day I ran my fourth Comrades marathon in 2014. It was a chilly Sunday morning at 5:00 am and all the athletes were lined up for a grueling 89 kilometer run from Pietermaritzburg to Durban. I lined up with 14,693 runners, all of us excited and nervous. The normal starting procedures were followed: the South African National Anthem was played followed by Chariot of Fire. With tears running down our faces, we awaited the starter's gun. We were off! We ran in initial darkness through the city of Pietermaritzburg towards the first obstacle of the day, Poly Shorts, a climb that warmed up the legs and took us up to Ashburton. Harrison Flats welcomed us and sent us on our way towards Inchanga, a hill big enough to cause some introspection of "why I am doing this race?".

On Inchanga, and a few kilometers from the official halfway mark at Drummond, the realization struck me. I am not prepared for Comrades! I was panting due to humidity, or perhaps just the reality of the demanding Comrades Marathon route that was staring me in the face. I had to regain some form of inward composure. Walking up the steep climbs, the tar hot under the soles of my shoes, past Drummond, I reached for my cellular phone, wanting to phone Lauren, my friend who lives on the route and was picking me up at the finish line in Durban. I wanted to quit, thinking of Paul, Erin, and Ross. Participating in many running and cycling endurance events, I have come to know myself in a deep sense. I never allow myself to think of the people I love up until the last ten kilometers, and then I allow tears of gratitude to flow and heal. At this moment, I was thinking of my loved ones, at 45 kilometers. This was too soon!

Walking and thinking of giving up is new to me. I've had to work hard and fight for every mark; personal victories always came at a high price. I was still walking uphill, my cellular phone now back in my pocket! Now Botha's hill. From the corner of my eye, I saw a spectator with a beer in his hand and instinctively moved closer to him. "Can I please have a sip of your beer?" I asked. Without a second's thought, he reached into his cooler and pulled out a new beer, saying "here you go, a new one for the road ahead."

Manna from heaven for a tired runner, a runner at her wits end. Drinking this gift (I don't enjoy beer) gave the necessary nutrients. After finishing half the can, I placed it strategically next to the road for the next runner who may be in need of a sip of beer. A few minutes later, a large group of runners, fondly known as a "bus," passed. Joining them helped me reach the last 17 kilometers. I finished the Comrades marathon with a few minutes to spare. The victory was not my position or even the medal, but knowing that the incessant prayer throughout the day and the loving grace of our Creator made it possible. He placed people on route to encourage, supply, and share the road. For this reason, the race received its name: Comrades!

Even in the moments when you feel down and out, persistence goes a long way. Don't give up! Always stay focused!

6. Vary approaches to achievement with creativity

When do we know that we have achieved in a certain competition or at work? What are the achievement criteria in 2018 compared to 1943? There is a huge difference. In the year 1943, the first computer was invented by J Presper Eckert and John Mauchly. The invention was undertaken at the University of Pennsylvania and they called it ENIAC. The ENIAC could fit into a small three-bedroom house, 167 square meters and weighing a staggering 45,359 kilograms. In 2018, I am typing in the luxury of a bed-and-breakfast retreat 280 kilometers away from home in a remote little town called Clarens on a laptop that fits into a back pack. The same amount of difference can be found when asking two people if they achieved success in their first year of university. For one student, passing with an average of 50% is a great achievement and he/she can't wait to go home and share the good news with family and friends. Social media will be used to proclaim the news even before reaching home. On the other hand, a student with an average mark of 89% will cry about the failure. The expectation was to be top of the class and they missed this achievement by 3%. Tests will be asked to be re-marked and the disappointment will persist for a number of days.

The point I am trying to make is that achievement is a personal experience that has to take into account various factors: our original goal, external pressures, expectations, and perceptions of what success is. These are deep, personal factors which are uniquely individual.

This takes me back to my third year as an undergraduate Physiotherapy student. I received the news that I had failed my external clinical examination the previous day, and I was shocked. Not only had I presented a patient who I knew, but I also really enjoyed treating his hand after an injury. I knew all too well it was risky to use a hand-injured patient for my examination because hand therapy is mostly a postgraduate specialist study area. I clearly did not realize how intricate the hand was and how specialized the assessment was, during my very young undergraduate training. I had to go for a re-examination the following week and, thankfully, passed, but the moral of this failure follows. From that day onwards, I have been fascinated with the human hand and hand therapy. I wanted to know more and studying the anatomy of the hand, hungry to know why I failed the exam. That perceived failure and sadness has resulted in me obtaining a Master's degree in hand rehabilitation and teaching postgraduate Occupational and Physiotherapist in the specialist field of hand therapy. That failure has positively changed me towards reading the Bible and wanting to know about the hands of Jesus, fueling my faith and my appreciation for the human body sculpted by the Creator.

What if the architect and Creator of our lives want to call us to an adventure, wants you to take a little gravel road that very few have traveled, to teach you, for your enjoyment, to have a life in abundance? He, the all-powerful Creator, may view achievement very differently to society norms.

Would you not consider viewing achievement differently? What about, after doing your utmost best in achieving your goals and performing somewhat under par, still be happy and praise the winner or console the person who failed?

7. Bounce back with flair

Once the setback has been felt, life has suddenly become real, the paw-paw has hit the proverbial fan. Feel the disappointment! We are human with emotions and tears. Allow yourself the freedom to feel it.

We are blessed with Erin, our beautiful and bright daughter. I encourage her to cry when she has had a bad day, but not at school. She climbs in the car, where she has a safe space to feel emotional if she needs to, and tells me about her day. It's okay to be sad when you have supportive friends, family, and colleagues who will be there. However, there is nothing worse than the opposite.

After the emotions have come out, let action follow. Ask logical questions about your area of strength, the external factors at play, and how it could have been approached differently. Then you have the luxury to bounce back with flair!

Do it better, do it with more passion and more of your personal style. You now have nothing to lose, so go for it!

Disclaimer to the above. I am assuming that your bouncing back act, if legal, is something that will benefit your company, is not a health risk to yourself and others, and hopefully will serve others.

CREATION OF LOVE: OVERCOMING SHAME

There are times when it is clear that we have messed up badly. Hurting family, friends, and others because of addictions, personal trauma, personality traits, and faults. Times when we have shame pumping through our veins in place of blood.

How to move forward amidst a wave of shame?

1. Acknowledge in writing, praying, and speaking

It is very healing to have the ability to acknowledge that an error has been made. The simple words "I am sorry" mean so much.

Deeply imbedded in the words "I am sorry" is the acknowledgement that a mistake was made, of which the person is not proud and feels that a wrong has been done to another. It's a bitter pill to swallow for the personal ego. The ego has to be tamed in order to be sorry and to communicate this into words.

For this reason, there are people in our lives who we cannot utter those words to. How can we look bad in front of others?

It takes a personal sacrifice to sincerely be sorry. To save a relationship and eventually be able to deeply love the people in your life, it is a necessary process which takes time. Starting the personal growth to be able to not only save relationships but have strong and healthy relationships takes prayer.

Communication with the Creator will open your heart's door and your mind to start thinking in a different way. Not the old way of thinking, but a clearer and healthier thought life. It, therefore, starts with thoughts. Ask God to bring about a change, to help you to mature and to grow into a person you can be proud of so that you can walk in a manner that, when you reflect on the progress achieved from where you started, you can truly say "I have worked hard," "I never gave up on myself," "my wife/husband/children/family is proud of me," I am a better friend," "I can love myself and others in a healthier way," and "my Creator is proud of me."

Prayer requires time, a commodity that is rare in a mad-rushed society where most things are convenient and requires little patience. Our Creator wants to spend time with us. Will you make the effort and accept His invitation?

Who is the one person that you would love to meet? It can be anyone anywhere in the world. So, you would like to meet the president of your country and have a conversation with him. The phone rings and his secretary has set aside an hour for a meeting. The only catch is that it is scheduled three hours from now and you have made prior plans. What will you do? Decline the invitation to meet the president or cancel your plans? I am convinced that the plans will be put aside. You may even get your hair cut, take a shower, put on your best outfit, and be at least 40 minutes early for the meeting.

In the attempt to gain more perspective, the Creator of the universe wants to spend time with you! Not the president, the Almighty, All-knowing God! The one being that loves you unconditionally and created you in your mother's womb. He has always wanted a close relationship with humans and it is a popular belief that this is the reason why He created human beings. We are created in His image to commune with Him.

How can we commune or have fellowship with Him? An equally difficult concept to explain to children. It is difficult to explain because we lack the childlike faith that is necessary to trust and believe in what we cannot see;

however deep this ability in us is, to have the faith to know that He is around us and He is in us, and we are created in the image of God.

A meeting needs the quiet that cannot be found in a busy office park or shopping mall. Having to make time when it is quiet and peaceful is a good start. Why not wake up before anyone else in your home when the sun is starting to wake up the world? Give your best to the Master: the best of your time, your energy, and your thoughts. Then, in the quiet moments, be still and present. When the mind starts thinking thoughts of what to do, who to call, a message that should be replied to, or a deadline that needs to be met, bring back your thoughts to the present. Don't be hard on yourself in this process of becoming still. Direct your thought to what you are thankful for. Breathe slowly in and slower out and relax your shoulders. Feel the thankfulness for another day, a healthy heart, and the air that moves in and out of your lungs. Life-sustaining air. It cannot be purchased! No amount of money can buy health. Your Creator, who you are spending time with, is not asking for your money, an increase in sales, or deadlines. He is asking you to just be, to be and to feel what is in His heart for you. Now, talk plainly to Him, praise Him, and tell Him. You will move closer to healing and, ultimately, to Love.

After meeting with God formally, now ask Him to be close to you in the day ahead with the decisions that need to be made and the people you may meet. Surely you can share with others why you are changing and how this process can be achieved.

Try your hand at writing what you have experienced from waking up and in your moments with God. It is very healing to write. Take it a step further and plan your goals in this manner.

Then it is time to go and acknowledge and ask for forgiveness. It may take a few days or weeks, but don't let it take too long. Words and deeds can cause much suffering in others. Stop the suffering as soon as possible. Talk to your wife, children, friends, family, or colleagues. Even if you say the words "I am sorry" and "please forgive me," it may not have the result you want. The anger and hurt may be deeper than the words can heal. Do it anyway! Even when you cannot meet with them face-to-face and make amends, do it over the phone or in a message (last option). Make sure the words are sincere and prepare for the lashing that may come your way, accept it, and hold your tongue to avoid causing more hurt. Take it! Stand there and feel the hurt. You are healing, and you are wanting only good for the other person. This may be a first in a self-consumed life.

Take a step back and give room and time! Now God can do the magic.

2. Forgive yourself

Asking for forgiveness is an important step; self-forgiveness is imperative. To forgive oneself is an abstract concept and is often undervalued. A reason for this difficult task may be the personal realization that you are capable of doing wrong.

Think back to your childhood experiences at home. How often Mom asked who was at fault for spilling the juice, breaking the window, or hurting a sibling? When she expected an answer, not one child took responsibility for the wrong. The point being made is that, from a young age, we find it difficult to acknowledge that we are capable of wrong actions.

After accepting that you are capable of the mistake, you are causing the hurt, and you are the reason for the tears of another, then the process of self-forgiveness can start.

3. Give to yourself what you want from others

The reason for hurting others can run deep, all the way back to childhood, in your parents' home, and with relationships between parents and siblings.

A sure way of knowing that you are living in the past and holding on to what you did not get from another is how your thoughts will frequently wander during the day, directed at a specific person or event.

Thoughts directed to undesired and negative feelings and events will affect your progress; it will act as a block. Love will not be easy when you feel you deserved more. An abusive father can negatively affect your thoughts and how you view love. No excuse is ever acceptable when an adult hurts a child. None! And believe me when I tell you that God detests the abuse. People have choices and freewill, this can be used positive or negative, and the decision does not rest with God. The abusive parent will have to bear the consequences, seen or unseen.

You may not know the love of a caring parent, and you may think about it daily. Feelings build up.

Your responsibility is to start changing thoughts. Not an easy task! With help and love, it is possible.

4. Kindness in self-talk

I remember when I started forgiving myself, realizing that my thoughts are holding me back from the life I was praying fervently for, a life where I can string together thoughts of goodness and kindness, thoughts far removed from the trauma of my younger days. These thoughts played over and over, like a movie or a song repeating itself, images and sounds holding my young mind back from discovering what is real and making sense about things around me.

It was only when I felt sick of the same movie playing involuntary in my mind that I realized I needed help. I was literally sick of myself. Negative thoughts are toxic! They are more destructive than a physical blow. They are an unseen poison affecting the personal psyche, a behavior-changing poison, altering the way we think about everything, including the people who love us. Their love is received with suspicion. Negative thoughts destroy relationships.

I reached that sick stage at 16 years of age, sick of myself and my thoughts when change is the only way forward; otherwise, it would be the end of me.

Change started with the way I talked to myself. Suddenly I awakened to the idea that I am not a passenger in the process of the repetitive movie. I was fueling it with the way I talked to myself. Silently, of course.

To suppress negative thoughts are not effective to bring about change. Suppressing the undesired self-talk and thoughts was not the answer. Replacing it, that was the answer! Having to become so aware of what I was thinking about and what I was saying to myself felt strange at first. I had to talk to myself kindly, replace negative words with positive ones. Consistency paid off. I started saying, "I will not give up on myself, I can love, I will grow, and I will get better!".

I was going to church, Sunday school and prayed while going through years of wrong thinking. Even in a church service, my thoughts kept wandering off, always negative. It is for this reason that I believe in the goodness and love of our Creator. He never gave up on me. He protected me and allowed people to love me unconditionally.

I was writing my final matric exam, and afterward, my friends and I celebrated the completion of our secondary schooling phase. My father, a layman pastor, was transferred. Our new congregation was 14 kilometers from our previous congregation. It was on the same evening of our celebrations that my parents attended a meeting in our new congregation. My life would never be the same.

On returning home, my dear parents waited for me. My mom could not wait to tell me that she met a very kind young man. He was our choir conductor. I thought it strange that she would tell me only about one member of the new congregation.

The next evening, a choir practice was scheduled, and I attended. Before the commencement, the vestry door opened, and a tall dark-haired man walked in. It was love at first sight. My eyes relayed the message that my heart instinctively knew. I was looking at my future husband at the age of 18. Paul walked into the church after giving a recorder lesson. I am unable to tell you who was with him or how many attended that recorder lesson. First impressions were made, how devoted he is, he is tall, with gorgeous blue eyes, loving eyes, so neat and clean. Don't laugh at me.

Fast-tracking forward. Knowing Paul for 20 years and being married to him for 16 years, he has literally loved me back to life. He is a precious gift from our Creator. He has loved me in my teens, twenties, and thirties.

The day I shared my heartache with Paul was a further catalyst for my healing and progress towards loving. Remembering the sobs and confession, I placed on him a burden that was heavy to carry. It was a burden too heavy for one to carry. Our Creator carried me up until that point, but He allowed a gentle, humble soul into my life. The healing was slow, but it was true and good.

5. Slow steps and fast steps towards your dream future

The slow, relentless, consistent forward motion towards your potential, I want this for you. The Creator desires this for you! Why? You have something to give to relieve the suffering of others. If you disagree on this point, then you are on the journey of love but perhaps still in the beginning phase.

When your thoughts are centered on your errors and the error of others, it is time to commence serious introspection.

What do you wish or dream about doing with your life? Is there something you regret not doing?

6. Be in nature

Make the time to be in nature. Even in a busy work schedule, be creative with planning. What about planning a walk-meeting in a nature reserve, close either to you or the person you are meeting? A nature reserve or even a park will provide a perfect setting for creative decision making, an opportunity to increase the heart rate and breathe deeper. For deep reflection, it is advisable to make time for walks in solitude.

Time in nature is not only healthy but also ensures a connection with the Creator.

7. Find the stillness

Stillness can be helpful to heal from a shameful experience. Stillness can be twofold. Firstly, it can be the absence of surrounding noises such as silencing the phone or switching off technology for a day. Secondly, it is a deeper stillness. This stillness refers to the absence of self-judging thoughts or replaying an incident over in your own mind.

8. Love

If a human being can dig deeper in searching of love that flows from God, the Creator of love and life, then it will be possible to have an eternity awaiting such a brave soul. Don't worry about the wrinkles under your eyes or on your thighs. Your age will be of no importance. No gender, race, religion, or culture will be the cause of judgement. Standing in front of the Almighty, face to face, with only how much you have loved Him and how much you have loved your neighbor, will determine your end.

Change is the only constant in life. This changing world can be appreciated when we take a glimpse back in history. World War I and II have come and gone. The economy has had its ups and downs. Leaders worldwide have lived, reigned, and have passed on. Human emotions move between highs and lows daily.

Is there any one thing that is constant in our existence as humans on Earth?

This is a question I have pondered for years. Now I can answer with a clear "yes!". There is one thing constant throughout all ages. Love!

This love letter will demonstrate aspects of love, such as its source and its flow. My intention is for you, as the reader, to discover your true love and live an eternal life even after your earthly one.

Genesis 2: 1-4

"Thus the heavens and the earth, and all the host of them, were finished. And on the seventh day God ended His work which He had done, and He rested on the seventh day from all His work which He had done. Then God blessed the seventh day and sanctified it, because in it He rested from all His work which God had created and made. This is the history of the heavens and the earth when they were created, in the day that the LORD God made the earth and the heavens,"

Has Jesus felt shame on Earth? Do you recall the days leading up to His crucifixion? The Son (Yahshua) experienced immense shame on the cross, and He was innocent.

PART V

The Creator loved the world so much that He gave His Son, who became flesh. His love was transformed in Yahshua, known as Jesus Christ in modern times and this is the reason why Part V received the name "The Second Creation - Jesus."

A love so big bestowed to human beings in the form of Jesus. Once this love is understood with a gut-like clarity, it will leave a human changed forever. An inward gaze will be replaced by an outward focus on others rather than one's own self. Opinions of being critical about exterior human appearances will disappear. You will be less focused on own emotions and feelings and be more inspired by this Love created and provided by the Creator in Jesus.

Lastly, Part V will conclude by documenting biblical writings of Paul, John, Matthew, Mark, and Luke as they travelled with Jesus. On their journeys, they provided beautiful insight of how Jesus demonstrated His love through His teachings and miracles.

Birds

SECOND CREATION: JESUS

Boldness beyond measure is bestowed upon me to be able to write about a concept that bridges times past and times to come. Love came before creation and will outlast creation and human existence. At the core of love is the love of God for creation and mankind. This is depicted by Him sending the Son.

Prophets proclaimed the One that will come to bruise the head of Satan. The One being prophesied to come and save humanity is Jesus Christ. God so loved the world that He will give His only Son. Recall the crucifixion of Christ! Christ dying on the cross was the ultimate act of love and God allowed His Son to die for mankind. That was love and is love for an eternity.

God's intention is made clear in the above paragraph. Man has fallen in the beginning of time in the Garden of Eden. Man listened to the lies of the snake (the devil) and, despite God's instruction to not eat the fruit of one of the trees in the luxurious Garden of Eden, decided to act on devious information provided to them.

Every human need was provided for in the Garden of Eden. Oxygen, shelter, human interaction, food, water, a peaceful environment, no stress, no threats, unpolluted air, and a view that must have been beautiful. God provided the best for His creation, like a father who provides the best for his children.

Satan told Adam and Eve that if they eat the fruit from the Tree of Good and Evil, they will possess the power of God. The disappointment was deep. Eating the fruit did not make them as powerful as God. Satan had deceived them; it had been a lie. Alas, God had wanted to protect humanity against Satan's lies and evil ways.

God did not punish Adam and Eve after they ate the forbidden fruit. Instead, what God wanted to protect Adam and Eve from was set in motion. This can be further illustrated when Adam and Eve realized they were naked and shyness set in for the very first time. They lost purity and innocence. It was simply the result of their actions and not a punishment by God.

Sharing a testimony may shed light on this topic of punishment. Pregnant with our first child and two weeks over the expected delivery date, my gynecologist advised me to come to the hospital so that an induction can be performed. Natural birth was the preferred initial step to get Erin into the world.

I was anxious weeks prior to this day as this was my child, my first experience of birth, the period God said would be painful for every woman after Eve's Garden of Eden moment of sin. Praying was my shield against fear. "God, please help me through natural labour; I am scared, and please help our little girl to be healthy". I prayed weekly, daily, hourly.

The induction was performed to speed up the labour process. Hours went by and the signs of labour started to show very slowly at first. 12 hours after induction, the only result was two centimeters of dilation. The medical team decided to speed up the process further with an intravenous drip. There was no difference in the pelvic floor dilation. However, due to the internal examination process, my water broke, an experience I am sure never to forget. After my water broke, the sisters put a foetal heart monitor around my abdomen to measure the contractions. Painful contractions are experienced by women daily and have for centuries, making childbirth painful and tiring. The readings on the monitor were staggering. They indicated that I was moving towards full labour, with fast contractions at increasing regular intervals. However, my body did not show the same readiness as dilation was still at two centimeters. Questions were asked about my pain levels and my answer was the same for each question: "I have no pain". On no medication and only the induction drip, I experienced absolutely no pain.

Shortly thereafter, I had a caesarean section with an epidural. The theatre sister made mention of The Garden of Eden. "You know, when God said woman will bear children in pain, He was very angry. He is not angry anymore. He has allowed research to provide pain relief in the form of an epidural. It will help you; please take it."

Erin was born. She was a beautiful, healthy, glowing baby girl. I gave thanks to God for His faithfulness, protection, and love. A modern-day miracle took place in our lives. Do you believe God can and will work in your life?

1 Corinthians 13:13
"And now abide faith, hope, love, these three; but the greatest of these is love."

The birth of Erin and the words of the sister who assisted me in the operating theatre shed new light on the concept of punishment by God. It is clear that punishment was part of the lives of people in the Old Testament, before the birth of Jesus.

When Jesus came to Earth, He had a very specific purpose. This purpose was to eradicate the idea of punishment by God. It was to take away a negative concept that kept people away from a close relationship with God and instill a new concept: the concept of love! How did Jesus obtain this purpose?

Firstly, Jesus was an avid student in the temple in Jerusalem. He spent hours in the temple learning from the teachers. In these learning periods, it was not enough for Him to listen, so He also asked questions. They must have been excellent questions because Jesus's questions and understanding astonished the people in the temple. Jesus was only 12 years old at the time.

Luke 2: 41-47

"His parents went to Jerusalem every year at the Feast of the Passover. And when He was twenty years old, they went up to Jerusalem according to the custom of the feast. When they had finished the days, as they returned, the Boy Jesus lingered behind in Jerusalem. And Joseph and His mother did not know it; but supposing Him to have been in the company, they went a day's journey, and sought Him among their relatives and acquaintances. So when they did not find him, they returned to Jerusalem, seeking Him. Now so it was that after three days they found Him in the temple, sitting in the midst of the teachers, both listening to them and asking them questions. And all who heard Him were astonished at His understanding and answers."

It was not only a teacher/student interaction in the temple. Jesus was actively engaged in the discussions surrounding God and His will. In these interactions where Jesus was educated, as a young boy, He felt at home. Mary and Joseph packed up their belongings and began to journey back home. Jesus was so focused on where He believed His time should be spent that He did not even ask permission to stay behind. He was confident and wanted to busy Himself in His Father's work.

STUDENT BECOMES A TEACHER

The engrossed student continued to grow and mature physically, cognitively, and, more importantly, spiritually. This maturation process culminated in Jesus becoming a Teacher. Jesus traveled, taught people, and performed miracles. He became a Master Teacher and people, hearing of the teachings, flocked to Him. The needy came to listen to Jesus. It is not only the content and actions of Jesus that made Him stand out, but the way He taught.

Jesus was a teacher who displayed love in all His teachings. I am reminded of a time period when God worked on my teaching methods. The Hand Amplified course is a hand-rehabilitation course that I was inspired to develop with dear friends of mine. It provides post-graduate education for Physiotherapist and Occupational therapist who have an interest in the human hand.

One of the courses was scheduled to be held in central South Africa, in the town of Bloemfontein. What made this course different was that I had to present more content than usual due to Jess not being able to attend and lecture. She has years of lecturing experience, unlike my measly four years of lecturing experience. I felt uneasy! I believed that God would provide the strength and insight for me to lecture both Jess's and my presentations. It would be a new experience to lecture for two and a half days. God provided help in the form of an Occupation Therapist who attended the course and helped with the practical sessions of splinting.

As I open the Bible app on my phone, I have a habit of closing my eyes and praying for a special verse from God. Holding true to this habit, I opened the app and closed my eyes, praying for support and help with the course ahead.

My finger clicked on the book, then on the chapter, and then on the verse.

The message I was given was a message on love. What did it mean? Did God want me to love the course? He wanted me to love the people attending the course! I then realized my focus had to be shifted.

The reason I felt uneasy was that I was focused on myself and not others. The privilege of standing in front of people who I have just met was of more value than my own egoistic concerns of how I would be perceived by them. To teach in love was a new concept to me! It ran so deep that I had to change and let go of my ego. It would be a special weekend in Bloemfontein that would change my ideas of teaching.

We traveled by car. I drove while my friend sat in the passenger seat. What I didn't tell you was that she had phoned me the day before to share the news that she had been diagnosed with bronchitis and had lost her voice. There was a possibility I would have to perform the practical sessions alone. Driving with my sick friend for 403 kilometers, I believed it would work out. The realization dawned on me that trust and faith in God would get me through this course and I would learn how to teach with love, as Jesus had taught with love.

The characteristics of teaching-in-love, which I learned from the Master during my two-and-a-half-day Bloemfontein course and still learn daily in my lecturing, follow.

Kindness

The teaching opportunities Jesus used naturally occurred on His journeys. He rarely had a meeting planned in advance and did not need to send out invitations to ensure a full audience would be present to make it worthwhile.

On one occasion, Jesus walked down a mountain, followed by many keen learners. The Teacher traveled through difficult terrain when He demonstrated a lesson in kindness to the followers.

Matthew 8: 1-3

"When He had come down from the mountain, great multitudes followed Him. And behold, a leper came and worshiped Him, saying, 'Lord, if You are willing, You can make me clean.' Then Jesus put out His hand and touched him, saying, 'I am willing; be cleansed.' Immediately his leprosy was cleansed."

The man with leprosy was ideally positioned for an encounter with Jesus. We don't know if this man heard the sound of the multitude and assumed that he was in their path. What we can know, without a doubt, is that people with leprosy were outcasts and could not associate with people in the towns. They were seen as unclean. This is the reason the man was in the mountains, far away from the judgement of society.

Leprosy was incorrectly seen as a highly contagious disease. Leprosy, Hansen's disease as it is known in modern times, affects the eyes, skin, and nerves. Left untreated, as in the time of Jesus, the damage to the nerves can result in paralysis of hands, feet, and other parts of the body. The skin is damaged with painful ulcers, and blindness can also occur. This amount of suffering was felt by the man with leprosy because there was no cure or treatment. As if it wasn't enough to be in pain, he had to walk on harsh mountain terrain with painful feet, exposed to the harsh elements. He also suffered from loneliness, a lack of contact with his family. With the belief that leprosy was contagious, people were scared to touch him. This incorrect belief made the Jewish society fearful of this disease and this led to a severe lack of kindness.

Jesus made His way down the mountain and saw the man. The man approached Jesus. Can you imagine what must have gone through the minds of the multitude of people?

The Teacher gave them a lecture about kindness. He did not use words but demonstrated how to be kind. He stretched out His hand and touched the sick man. Jesus was not worried about being infected. Jesus was perhaps moved by compassion for the people who suffered under wrong perceptions. His actions shattered the untrue belief

Kindness was shown by reaching out to a person who was hurting and suffering. Love preceded this miracle of healing by a simple touch of the hand. The lesson I learned from this is to love others by being kind.

Transformation through love

The healing of the leprosy-sick man was a miracle. A bigger miracle that day on the mountain was the transformation of the multitude of followers who witnessed Jesus's teaching. The miracle referred to is the transformation of people's opinions and thoughts.

Transformation must be defined to ensure clarity of understanding. The word "form" implies the physical world surrounding us, including our physical body. Form can be extended to include the boundaries we experience in life. Think, for example, about the invisible border that separates one state or province from the neighboring area in your country. We talk about these boundaries as if they are physical restrictions. In the physical body, this invisible boundary was encountered by leprosy sufferers where they were physically off-bounds to society. The word "trans" is a prefix that can be defined as going beyond or soaring above. Transformation thus implies going beyond physical boundaries and forms. Jesus, through His teaching methods, successfully transformed the perception of physical boundaries imposed on people with leprosy and the pre-existing opinions of the crowd who following Jesus.

The transformation of body and mind was only possible through love, kindness, and dampening of the ego.

Humbleness

Jesus displayed the characteristic of humbleness in His teaching methods.

Matthew 8: 4

"And Jesus said to him, 'See that you tell no one...'"

Jesus, the humble Teacher, displayed an attitude of modesty after performing a miracle. The man was told he should make sure to tell no-one about what had happened on the mountain. Surely, we can argue that healing a man of leprosy with a touch and words is spectacular. Even in our modern, advanced, technology-rich world, no human can perform this miracle. We are creative and inventive, but we do not possess the capacity to heal someone with a mere touch.

The difference lies in the attitude. There are many inspirational people who have remained modest and humble: Nelson Mandela, Mother Teresa, Mahatma Gandhi, to name but a few. They understood the powerful teaching through humbleness inspired by a transformation of love. However, there are many living people who display a high-minded attitude and egoistic behavior for acts that cannot stand against anything as awesome as the miracle performed by Jesus.

There is power in humbleness.

Call to action

The now healthy man was given a call to action.

Matthew 8: 4

"...but go your way, show yourself to the priest, and offer the gift that Moses commanded, as a testimony to them."

It was the man's responsibility to escape not only from the physical boundary of the mountain but from the emotional boundary of solitude, loneliness, and suffering. According to the laws of the time, the man had to present himself to the priest before he could return to his family and re-join society. Before the restrictions of the law could be removed from a person suffering with leprosy, the priest had to certify that the person was cleansed. As an avid Jew, Jesus was aware of this law.

The man was instructed to take a gift with him and offer it, the giving of a gift as Moses commanded. It is clear that Moses institutes the procedures of cleansing and that it was not God. God was not responsible for ostracizing leprosy-sick citizens. This will be the testimony brought by the man to not only the priest but also to the leaders and Pharisees.

The kind and transformational Teacher not only healed a desperate man, to which the followers bore witnesses, but also succeeded to teach the priest, leaders, and Pharisees of the time. At that time, the local authorities, temple personnel, and leaders were aware of Jesus and His teachings because He was a former scholar in their midst. He has probably their best scholar, and the scholar had become the teacher. Jesus proclaimed a different teaching.

Allow me to explain the teachings of Jesus with more clarity. What can be clearer than reflecting on the scriptures of men who walked with Jesus on His journeys of teaching through love? The following chapters will explain the teachings of Jesus through the eyes, ears, and hearts of John, Matthew, Mark, and Luke, including short descriptions of the faithful companions of Jesus. The first chapter will be based on Paul's journeys. Paul vehemently proclaimed the teaching of Jesus. However, he never had the opportunity to travel with Jesus, unlike John, Matthew, Mark and Luke.

LOVE ACCORDING TO PAUL

Apostle Paul underwent a total transformation. He was called Saul of Tarsus by the Jews and was an avid soldier and leader of the Roman army. It was to Roman soldiers, under Saul's command, that many Christian followers lost their lives. To put it plainly, Saul was one of the most hated men among the Christians because of his persecution of the early disciples of Jesus. Until one day…

Saul was on a mission from Jerusalem to Damascus to arrest Jesus's followers and return them to Jerusalem. En route, he observed a great light. It was Jesus in His resurrected form after the crucifixion. Saul was blinded for three days. Jesus asked Saul why he was persecuting HIM?

After three days, symbolic when considering the three days before Jesus's resurrection, Saul started preaching the Gospel of Jesus of Nazareth. This was a complete conversion of purpose after being blinded.

Ananias of Damascus restored his vision and Apostle Paul was a changed man. Not only did he dedicate his time and life to preaching and furthering the Gospel of Jesus, but some say he authored thirteen (seven undisputed) of the twenty-seven books of the New Testament. His upbringing in the Roman Empire served him well and he had the education to write and speak clearly for his contributions to the Bible, a guide that is still read by people, believers or nonbelievers. Secrets of the Bible have become quotes among the secrets of wealth and success. Even leadership guides have been written by authors who have used concepts from the Bible.

The contributions of Paul have been so immense that it is only correct to learn from him and dissect what he has to say about love.

Paul was a devoted follower, writing these beautiful biblical versus about love.

1 Corinthians 2:9

"But as it is written; "Eye has not seen, nor ear heard, nor have entered into the heart of man the things which God has prepared for those who love Him".

1 Corinthians 13:1-8

"Though I speak with the tongues of men and of angels, but have not love, I have become as sounding brass or a clanging cymbal. And though I have the gift of prophesy, and understand all mysteries and all knowledge, and though I have all faith, so that I could remove mountains, but have not love, I am nothing. And though I bestow all my goods to feed the poor, and though I give my body to be burned, but have not love, it profits me nothing. Love suffers long and is kind; love does not envy; love does not parade itself, is not puffed up; does not behave rudely, does not seek its own, is not provoked, thinks no evil; does not rejoice in iniquity, but rejoices in the truth; bears all things, believes all things, hopes all things, endures all things. Love never fails. But whether there are prophecies, they will fail; whether there are tongues, they will cease; whether there is knowledge, it will vanish away."

LOVE ACCORDING TO JOHN

John, fondly known as the "Beloved Disciple" or the "disciple who Jesus loved", was the youngest Apostle and the only Apostle believed to have died from natural causes. He authored the Gospel of John, the three epistles of John, and, lastly, Revelations.

He was born in Bethsaida and his brother, James, was also one of the Apostles. He was also known as John of Patmos, John the Elder, and John the Evangelist.

John 3:16

"For God so loved the world that He gave His only begotten Son, that whoever believes in Him should not perish but have everlasting life."

Thousands of years after the creation, the world was in trouble. Sin had taken over man and another plan had to be made. The Creator loved the creation and human beings to such an extent that He sent His Son to earth. The Creator has not given up on mankind. In this sinful state, the Creator knew mankind would perish. The Son is a gift of love to the world, a sacrifice to humanity to bestow hope, overcome sin, and eventually serve for a greater good.

John 3:19

"And this is the condemnation, that the light has come into the world, and men loved darkness rather than light, because their deeds were evil."

Alas! Even after the Son was given to the world, men loved darkness more than light. The allure from the darkness was more attractive. Darkness leads to evil deeds, unlike love where kindness, giving, and caring for another are characteristics. Darkness was chosen. Characteristics of darkness are egoistic, self-seeking, killing, stealing, power-driven, and greed. The deeds of the people were evil.

John 3:35

"The Father loves the Son, and has given all things into His hand."

A light in the darkness was created and the Son illuminated the minds, hearts, and understanding of many because all things were given into His hand. No amount of evil could dampen the light from the Son. He had nothing to prove and was bold enough to teach in Jerusalem.

John 5:42

"But I know you, that you do not have the love of God in you."

The Son spoke his purpose in truth and conviction. It takes an unrelenting faith and conviction of purpose to teach so boldly. What was the prerequisite or the measurement that the Son used on the Pharisees and scribes? The presence or absence of Godly love! The Son looked at the deeds of the Pharisees and scribes and perhaps felt that there was an absence of love.

John 8:42

"Jesus said to them, "If God was your Father, you would love Me, for I proceeded forth and came from God; nor have I come of Myself, but He sent Me."

When a human being is filled with the love of the Creator, the ego will be tamed. The Creator's purpose placed in the heart will be the driving force, directing motivation that leads to deeds of light. Seeking to have a good and abundant life is perfectly fine.

John 10:17

"Therefore My Father loves Me, because I lay down My life that I may take it again."

Eternal life will be the gift for those who can gain an understanding in this teaching. Only the Creator and the Son are perfect. We fight evil daily. No human can claim to be only light and good. All that is needed to live in the love is to decide to seek the light amidst the darkness.

John 12:25

"He who loves his life will lose it, and he who hates his life in this world will keep it for eternal life."

Choose thoughts of light and love. The only commandment taught by the Son can be encapsulated in one. Love! It is not the Ten Commandments given to Moses. Just love!

John 14:21

"He who has My commandments and keeps them, it is he who loves Me. And he who loves Me will be loved by My Father, and I will love him and manifest Myself to him."

LOVE ACCORDING TO MATTHEW

Matthew, an Apostle of Jesus, is also known as Saith Matthew. The meaning of Matthew in Arabic is 'Gift of YHVH', a gift from the Creator Himself. Matthew was one of the four evangelists and also one of the twelve apostles commissioned by Jesus.

Born in Capernaum, Matthew walked with Jesus and wrote about His works on Earth and how we should love our neighbor.

Matthew 5:43-44

"You have heard that it was said, 'You shall love your neighbour and hate your enemy. But I say to you, love your enemies, bless those who curse you, do good to those who hate you, and pray for those who spitefully use you and persecute you,"

Wait a minute! Are you telling me, Matthew, that Jesus is teaching me to love my enemies? People who curse me should be blessed by my mouth? I must do good to people who hate me? My prayer should include those who use and persecute me? These are pretty high standards, especially in the modern times in which we live where it is so easy to block a person with the touch of a button on a screen, comment unfairly, share hateful and untrue comments, all on social media at anytime, anywhere. Not face to face!

Yes, Jesus wants us to love, bless, do good, and pray for the enemy. Two questions come to mind. Why does He want me to do that? How can I, a sinner myself, successfully do this? With sincerity and intentionally!

The question of "why" gets answered in the same bible reference.

Matthew 5: 45

"that you may be sons of your Father in heaven; for He makes His sun rise on the evil and on the good, and sends rain on the just and on the unjust."

Jesus loved, blessed, was compassionate and displayed kindness on Earth. He came to Earth as an example of a life where it was possible to love His enemy. Do you recall how He was persecuted unfairly and sentenced to be crucified? How He invited Judas to the Last Supper even though He knew the betrayal that would take place where Judas accepted silver coins to tell the authorities where they could find Jesus? Where He prayed on the cross asking God to forgive them because they do not know what they are doing?

Have you ever been sentenced unjustly and crucified? Surely not. Reality check, you are still alive if you are reading this. We will rarely have to go through what Jesus went through. In history, there have been faithful followers of Jesus and other religions who have had to die for what they believe in. These brave human martyrs lost their lives, like Jesus did, for a purpose bigger than themselves.

God is so good to His creation that we are mostly protected, with some challenging days in between. God cannot help Himself to be good to His creation. Two beautiful examples are given in the form of a sunrise and a rainfall.

Matthew 5: 46-48

For if you love those who love you, what reward have you? Do not even the tax collectors do the same? And if you greet your brethren only, what do you do more than others? Do not even the tax collectors do so? Therefore you shall be perfect, just as you Father in heaven is perfect."

Matthew 22:37

"Jesus said to him, 'You shall love the Lord your God with all your heart, with all your soul, and with all your mind.'"

Love with your entire being; your heart, soul, and mind. These three dimensions of love are talked about in the verse.

Matthew 22:39

"And the second is like it: 'You shall love your neighbour as yourself.'"

How much do you love yourself? Do you love yourself? If you have not reached a point of healthy self-love, loving a fellow human being is a difficult task. Without self-love, loving God and neighbor is virtually impossible.

Matthew 24:12

"And because lawlessness will abound, the love of many will grow cold."

Who is the author of lawlessness? The evil one, the fallen angel, the devil. The devil wants company in the eternal fire that awaits him after the return of Jesus. The continued attempt of the evil one to cause souls to stumble perpetuates lawlessness among mankind. Do not be ignorant! The fight between good and evil is real. Know this and stop his attempts to destroy your soul and your family. How will you know that the devil is working in your life? Your love for God and your neighbor will grow cold and love will be a trivial concept to you. Words that will be found in your vocabulary will be "me" and "I".

LOVE ACCORDING TO MARK

Saint Mark, the Evangelist, who was born in Cyrene 68 AD and was a Libyan, wrote the Gospel of Mark. According to Hippolytus, Mark belonged to a group of seventy disciples who were commissioned by Jesus to proclaim the gospel in Judea.

Mark became a companion to Peter when their paths crossed somewhere between Antioch, Asia, and Rome. Mark made a good travel companion and acted as an interpreter to Peter. The sermons Peter gave along his travels were written down in the Gospel of Mark. Thereafter, Mark went to Cyprus with Barnabas after the Jerusalem Council.

Mark is known to have founded the church of Alexandria 19 years after Jesus ascended. The church of Alexandria is known today as the Greek Orthodox Church of Alexandria.

Teach us about love, Mark.

Mark 1:11

"Then a voice came from Heaven, 'You are My beloved Son, in whom I am well pleased.'"

Mark 10:21

"Then Jesus, looking at him, loved him, and said to him, 'One thing you lack: Go your way, sell whatever you have and give it to the poor, and you will have treasure in heaven; and come, take up the cross, and follow Me.'"

We work hard for money to pay bills, homes, and that special vacation. Hard work is honorable and very important. Why then did Jesus tell the rich young man that he is still missing one thing? Jesus told him he was lacking in one area, even though he did much good and obeyed all the commandments. Everything this man earned and acquired in his young life had to be sold and the profits were to be given to the poor. This was too much to ask, and the man walked away. The youngster was wise enough to ask Jesus what he should do to inherit eternal life. Some things are just too difficult. Have you been instructed by Jesus to sell all your possessions and give it to the poor? Perhaps your life has been dedicated to ministry and you have sacrificed much. I am of the belief that, if you are going to ask Jesus to change your life and you live a life centered around the commandment of love set out by Jesus, you will be instructed to ensure your Earthly needs, wants, and desires are not more important than a life of servanthood.

Difficult concepts indeed, yet more freeing and peaceful than most things we experience on Earth. The freedom and peace will allow you to operate and make your next move in the spiritual dimension. You will discover why you were created and pursuing your passion will ultimately serve others and provide a great sense of fulfilment.

Pick up your cross! It will not be an easy road that always makes sense. You will be questioned, ridiculed, and mocked for pursuing your passion. It will be hard to carry your cross. The evil one will try and orchestrate you to think two things. "Who do you think you are? You cannot achieve this; it is too big for you". Accept this, pick up your cross anyway, and move forward with Jesus. One foot in front of another, step by step. He will guide you! Trust Him!

Mark 12:30-31

"And you shall love the Lord you God with all your heart, with all your soul, with all your mind, and with all your strength. This is the first commandment. And the second, like it, is this: You shall love your neighbour as yourself. There is no other commandment greater than these."

To love our neighbor as we love ourselves? The question is do we love ourselves? A healthy self-love, grounded in confidence, kindness and care. If we possess these attributes, then we will have love to share with others. However, if we do not love ourselves and struggle to even like ourselves, we are in trouble and will find it very difficult to share love for another and, ultimately, for God. For this reason, I believe that we are instructed to love God first. To love God with all your heart, mind, soul, and strength, you will be able to love yourself in a healthy manner. He will change you, suppress your ego, and allow you joy and happiness which you can then share freely, with no expectations. Love will be the only reason to give to your neighbor.

You can trust the phrase that says there is no greater commandment than this! You can obey every aspect of your religion. Trust me; you can please don't hesitate. However, if you don't love your Creator with you entire heart, mind, soul, intellect, and strength and omit to love your neighbor as you love yourself, you will have done it all in vain.

Mark 12:33

"And to love Him with all the heart, with all the understanding, with all the soul, and with all the strength, and to love one's neighbour as oneself, is more than all the whole burnt offerings and sacrifices.

Love God with all your heart. Now that you know so much more about the anatomy and physiology of the heart, can you love with your whole heart? With every beat…love! On average, love 80 times a minute! Love even when you are asleep because your heart still beats. In times of excitement and joy, your heart beats faster. Will you then love more? When you're angry or sad, your heart still beats. Then still love God!

Love with all your understanding, from the knowledge and understanding you have acquired in school, in university, general knowledge, post-graduate level, and life-experience. Love God with it all. All this talk about knowledge makes me think. At times, knowledge can influence faith and ultimately draw us closer or push us further away from God and His love. There may seem like unrelated concepts. However, it can be seen in our fast-paced, science-packed world. Science and the unrelenting search for new discoveries are at the core of human existence. We want to know more. However, if we search and love God with our whole understanding, miracles happen. He is the creator of Heaven and Earth. He is all-knowing and what is wise with mankind is foolish with God.

The discovery of the God-gene is a miraculous discovery. Is this gene, the vesicular monoamine transporter 2, a sign of God and His love in the creation of Man? Can it be compared to the signature of an artist putting a signature on his or her personal painting? The hypothesis states that this God-gene predisposes humans to spirituality.

A new human life birthed after the intimacy of love reveals another miracle. At this moment in time, 7.7 billion miracles from God walk the Earth with many souls who have passed before us. The faithful love of God has never failed mankind. It is our understanding, at times limited, that draws us away from this all-encompassing love. Even if you don't believe in the Creator YHWH or Yahshua, every cell in your body craves to know Him. It is born in you, inseparable by your culture, understanding, or belief.

Love Him with all your soul. If there was ever a concept that was difficult to fathom, the soul is it. I am reminded of my six-year-old son Ross asking me about the soul. Let me confess that it was not an easy answer. I fumbled over words I have tried to understand since the age of 13.

To be able to love with your soul, you need to know that you don't only have a soul but you are a soul. You are flesh and blood. You are a spiritual esoteric being because you have the traces, in every cell of your body, of the Creator, who we cannot see but can experience in a different domain of existence.

Ross's question was if we would recognize each other once we die and meet Yashua. The transformation from flesh to soul can only be described as Spiderman from human to superhero. We will be transformed, and we will take on a new body in which our souls will fit perfectly, a heavenly body clothed in white array. Earthly needs, desires, and pains will be left behind. A future for which the preparation will be completed on Earth awaits us. You see, what causes us to stumble and worry on Earth is deeper than our flesh and blood. Incorrect thoughts influence our thought patterns, affecting our actions, and eventually change our attitude, beliefs, and character. It changes who we are and affects the soul. How do you know if your Earthy preparation for your transformation to a superhero is not going so well? Worry, stress, anxiousness about the future, feeling distant from God, and lack of trust in God; a separation from your spiritual Creator. You will feel that something is not right!

The good news is that Yashua gave us the ultimate advantage against any form of evil or negative thoughts! It is a daily endeavor, but we can improve. With these simple words, you can start the healing process. "God I don't know what to do and do not want to do anything without You, help me." This is the first step to love Him with your soul.

Love Him with all your strength. This indicates that your energy and power is given to you, daily, to love. Love God and love your neighbor. What then? What happens when you have given all your strength and you have none left? Then He will take over and give you the rest.

Jeremiah 29: 13

"And you will seek Me and find Me, when you search for Me with all your heart."

Strength is a gift provided by Him. Oxygen provided through every breath, circulating from the lungs into every cell through the flow of blood. It nourishes the muscles to contract in response to the central and peripheral nervous system's command. If your brain does not get oxygen, your body will not function. Oxygen is God's gift to us. Is it then too much to ask to give to Him all our strength in love?

LOVE ACCORDING TO LUKE

Luke, one of four early evangelists, is often referred to as a physician, one that heals, and also a disciple of Paul. Luke was born in the Roman Empire. His upbringing served him well when one considers his literacy contributions to the Bible. The Gospel of Luke, as well as Acts of the Apostles, are attributed to him, as author, by early church fathers. Although contested by some, over a quarter of the New Testament was written by Luke, more than any other writer of the Bible.

Luke received the name Saint Luke the Evangelist. In his evangelistic duties, it was believed that he accompanied Paul on many missions to spread the gospel and it is believed by some that Luke paid the ultimate price. Luke died 84 AD near Boeotia, Greece, as a martyr. He was hanged from an olive tree, although this is disputed.

The Evangelist Luke wrote verses which were deep and profound. They touch my core and give deep peace in a whirlwind of thoughts about life and love.

Luke 12:2

"For there is nothing covered that will not be revealed, nor hidden that will not be known."

Luke's insight into truth holds true to the current situation in the rainbow nation of South Africa. The truth is spilling out. The injustices that occurred in the past, during the apartheid era, abuse against young males and females, truth about political fraud and state capture attempts, mismanagement in state entities. Luke's words sound like a prophesy coming true. Social media has made it almost impossible to hide things and has made the borders of Mother Earth smaller.

Behaviors: abuse, fraud, deception, dishonesty, theft, and murder. Do we still possess love? What happens to love in this environment? Is love present in politics, in government entities, in business, our country, and our homes?

It is crystal clear that the teaching of Yahshua was, and is, about love. The New Testament is truly a love-letter to believers.

Consolation is found in the following verse.

Luke 12:4-7

"And I say to you, My friends, do not be afraid of those who kill the body, and after that have no more that they can do. But I will show you whom you should fear: Fear Him who, after He has killed, has power to cast into hell; yes, I say to you, fear Him! Are not five sparrows sold for two copper coins? And not one of them is forgotten before God. But the very hairs of your head are all numbered. Do not fear therefore; you are of more value than many sparrows."

At times, fear is part of our existence and, with the behaviors and actions mentioned above, it is clear why. The news is full of negative information. However, we are instructed not to fear any human because God's caring eye is on the sparrows that are sold for a minimal price. Do not fear! Take courage to heart! God knows the plans He has for your life. Fear only that you are not living His plan for your life.

Luke 3:22

"And the Holy Spirit descended in bodily form like a dove upon Him, and a voice came from heaven which said, 'You are My beloved Son; in You I am well pleased."

In this beautiful bible verse written by Luke, he speaks about God affirming Jesus. Why do you think God affirmed His Son? God affirmed Jesus with two concepts. The first is to convey and speak your love to another. "You are My beloved Son" is a direct and soft way to speak His love. In this, it can be appreciated that the author of life and love deemed it a necessity to speak His love. It is my belief that God also strengthened Jesus by sharing His love in this verbal comment. Love, when expressed sincerely, can strengthen! What does love strengthen? It strengthens persistence to enable the achievement of a goal, a goal that requires courage and personal sacrifice.

A faithful Shephard in my church congregation has said, on several occasions, that we can only connect the dots from the past. We can connect the dots of Jesus's life by reflecting on His last days on Earth. His attitude is admirable. Consider the reality He faced in Jerusalem. His purpose was misunderstood by the Jews of the time. He was supposed to free them from the yoke of oppression, paying high taxes and being mistreated, and resources were scarce. However, Jesus did not free them from their oppressors and high taxes. Jesus was welcomed into Jerusalem as a king. Later, He was crucified. He suffered on a cross for the sins of humankind. How was He able to still serve up until the day he was crucified? I believe His attitude and servanthood towards fulfilling His life purpose was achieved because of the love of His Father. God's love sustained and strengthened Him until his last day.

The second aspect, "in You I am well pleased", shows positive feedback lifts you up. These words were spoken before completion of the task Jesus was commissioned to perform on Earth. Yes, Jesus knew what was awaiting Him on the cross. He wasn't ignorant about His ending. God's love and positive attitude towards Him uplifted and blessed Him. Should we not love and uplift?

PART VI

The final part includes chapters titled: "Love of the Vine" and "Love in the Trinity". The creativity of the Creator has never stopped. Through Jesus, the creation of love was brought to Earth as a gift to humanity.

LOVE OF THE VINE

John 14:30-31

"I will no longer talk much with you, for the ruler of this world is coming, and he has nothing in Me. But that the world may know that I love the Father, and as the Father gave Me commandment, so I do. Arise, let us go from here."

To know your end and still choose to live your purpose takes courage. This was the courage He demonstrated before His death on the cross. The text referenced above is an apt demonstration of the opposites encountered in life. Jesus talks about "the ruler of the world is coming" as an indication that Satan is out to get Him, the fight between good and evil, but Jesus opposed the lures of Satan until His end, and now He can say "he has nothing in Me." A call to wake up is made. The evil one is also out to get us, deceive, lie, and destroy. Destroying relationships and personal growth is Satan's superpower. He does not care about human beings because no love can be found in him. The intentions of the evil one is self-serving. He does not want to suffer his demise alone. Knowing he will burn in an eternal fire seems a little better if he can recruit as many humans as possible to accompany him.

What did Jesus use to destroy the evil one's temptations? The words of the creator and Love. The intention of Jesus, however, was always clear. He spoke openly to the disciples, with more urgency prior to the crucifixion day. The intention of Jesus has always been to be faithfully connected to the purpose of LOVE in serving others.

John 15: 6-7

"If anyone does not abide in Me, he is cast out as a branch and is withered; and they gather them and throw them into the fire, and they are burned. If you abide in Me, and My words abide in you, you will ask what you desire, and it shall be done for you.

We should abide in Jesus. Abide is an interesting word. It is a do-word or verb. However, it is an acceptance, obeying, or upholding of someone's ideals or decisions. Abiding in Jesus then surely means that we are encouraged to uphold His teachings performed on Earth. We are encouraged to read, meditate on, and act according to the words spoken by Jesus, as written in the Bible by His faithful disciples. The punishment for not abiding is the same as the evil one, a fiery ending. It gives me more pleasure to share the reward with you. Our best attempts to abide in Jesus will be rewarded.

A secret is shared. This will change your life and the lives of your loved ones. In searching and endeavoring to abide in Jesus, you will be rewarded with the desires of your heart and whatever you ask will be effortlessly allowed into your life. Can this be true? Yes, it is written in the Bible, the spoken words of Jesus.

In sharing this secret, I want to assure you of the good intentions of Jesus towards you. What are the desires you have? Are they desires that will only serve you, to build your wealth to afford the car or house or jet you always wished you had? If you have abided in Jesus and asked Him for this, then, if the secret holds true, you must already have the car, house, and jet. Then why are you not yet the owner of these? It is not the secret that is not true! That is a given; nobody can dispute this. Perhaps abiding in Jesus is more difficult than we believe. Abiding in Jesus and His words will cause a transformation. The transformation will be an inside job. It will dig into the deepest fibers and cells of your being. It will alter you at a cellular level and transform your genetics in a figurative form. Once touched by the words and love of Jesus, a person transforms. Once transformed, the desires of such a person are different. The desires are directed outward rather than inward. Desires for others take center stage. Wanting to do good for others becomes the primary goal. A life lived for others in love fuels the desires. When you have reached this stage, after abiding in Jesus, ask whatever you desire, and it will be given to you, flowing into your life effortlessly, gifted by the Creator.

This is what I call the true-happiness zone.

John 15: 8-11

By this My Father is glorified, that you bear much fruit; so you will be My disciples. As the Father loved Me, I also have loved you; abide in My love. If you keep My commandments, you will abide in My love, just as I have kept My Father's commandments and abide in His love. These things have I spoken to you, that My joy may remain in you, and that your joy may be full.

After abiding in the words of Jesus, which are ultimately words inspired by the Creator, you will be fruitful. You will produce, create, give to others, show more sincere love in action and deed towards others, and be present in every moment with your children, friends, and spouse. This will, in turn, affect what energy returns to you. A life of fruitfulness is a life worth living. Reach this, dear reader! It takes constant effort, good daily routines, and giving the best of your time to Jesus.

John 15: 12-13

This is My commandment, that you love one another as I have loved you. Greater love has no one than this, than to lay down one's life for his friends.

Never has something been asked of us, by Jesus, that He has not been performed or tried first. Love as I loved you! Love others as Jesus loved you. How much does He love you? He loved us so dearly that He was pinned to a wooden cross. The pins were placed through His wrists and feet. Excruciating pain was experienced on the cross.

Why did Jesus give His life for us? Nobody has demonstrated the words "no greater love" more than Jesus, who laid down His life for His friends. Hanging on the cross was a self-sacrificial act of love. Do you recall the earlier reference to the evil one who is coming? Jesus knew the evil one has powers to betray and deceive all human beings who have ever lived and who will still be born. Hanging as an innocent Man on the cross without reproach, anger, or hatred towards His persecutors demonstrated the truest form of love. This love destroyed Satan and freed us of guilt.

John 15: 14-17

You are My friends if you do whatever I command you. No longer do I call you servants, for a servant does not know what his master is doing; but I have called you friends, for all things that I heard from My Father I have made known to you. You did not choose Me, but I chose you and appointed you that you should go and bear fruit, and that your fruit should remain, that whatever you ask the Father in My name He may give you. These things I command you, that you love one another."

It is an important point to make that we cannot choose Jesus. Once a person has given so much love to you, whether you accept this as true or not, surely it is not a choice to accept the person. He has given love so true for all mankind. He has chosen you! Embrace it and love Him and others as hard as possible. The last commandment is to LOVE!

Romans 8:37

"Yet in all these things we are more than conquerors through Him who loved us."

Preceding this verse, Paul wrote that they were killed all day long for Christ's sake and they were counted as sheep to be slaughtered. Amid the suffering, it appears that Paul took it like a man, standing after the blows were dealt and doing it with a great attitude.

What gave Paul the strength to persist in following and proclaiming the gospel of Christ?

He inspires and proclaims that he, with apostles, disciples, evangelists, and us, is a conqueror because of the love of Christ. Wow!? Can love make us conquerors in the face of severe tribulation?

The ultimate creation of the Creator is Love! The agape kind of Love displayed in the life and walk of Jesus Christ.

Sitting and typing this last chapter, I realize that Paul's words in Romans 8 are, in fact, a creative miracle that has sustaining power which can give us strength in hardships, distress, trauma, loss, poverty, and the suffering that life brings.

Romans 8:38-39

"For I am persuaded that neither death nor life, nor angels nor principalities nor powers, nor things present nor things to come, nor height nor depth, nor any other created thing, shall be able to separate us from the love of God which is in Christ Jesus our Lord."

When we realize how much we are loved by the Creator, the trinity (God the Father, Christ the Son, and the Holy Spirit) life can be truly magical. A turnaround is just around the corner, a new life. Any dream and passion can be pursued successfully.

Christ's love has been given freely on the cross for all mankind, living and dead. It crosses all ages and centuries. Now you must accept this love. After accepting the love, we will be able to agree with Paul that nothing can separate us from the love of our Creator. Whether we live or die, we will be surrounded by Christ's love. Fear not! No created thing can separate us from the love of God portrayed in Jesus Christ!

LOVE IN THE TRINITY

A question remains to be answered. How can I love the Creator? It is indeed a question that I want to answer with bold creativity while not making the answer too complicated.

Walking from my car, parked in the parking lot of my new work at the University of the Witwatersrand, the morning has been characterized by an overwhelming gratefulness for a life I love, knowing that God has bestowed blessings beyond measure upon me in the past year. Walking closer to the entrance of the office block, the realization dawns on me. Love the Creator in the Creation!

This is how I can love the Creator! I will be thankful when I walk past the green gardens of the University. During my afternoon run, I will stop at the rose garden of my neighbor and smell the roses, taking in the sweet scent and praising the Creator. I will wake up earlier in the morning, watch the mighty sun rise in the east, and give thanks for a new day. I will sit for a few minutes each day in silence and find stillness. I will use the mind I have been given to think of how good the Creator is. Perhaps all we need to love the Creator is to become more mindful of what is around us daily in the Creation!

Breathing life-giving oxygen allows the heart to transport oxygenated blood to sustain the body. Fill up on the breath of life the Creator has provided, every day.

I can show my love to the Creator by loving each student I am privileged to teach. Let me teach with love, as Jesus did! Teaching with love!

Looking at the people in my life through eyes of love, I wish to appreciate them more. I appreciate Paul like never before, a partner who has been a blessing from the Creator. I listen to and play with Erin and Ross, watching how they grow as healthy, energetic children. These are true blessings created. Let me love my family and friends. Let me be true in my love towards them. I am sincerely loving them and sending love to the other 7.7 billion of inhabitants on Mother Earth. I have come full circle and give back to the Creator, the Creator of love.

ABOUT
KHARIS PUBLISHING

KHARIS PUBLISHING is an independent, traditional publishing house with a core mission to publish impactful books, and channel proceeds into establishing mini-libraries or resource centers for orphanages in developing countries, so these kids will learn to read, dream, and grow. Every time you purchase a book from Kharis Publishing or partner as an author, you are helping give these kids an amazing opportunity to read, dream, and grow. Kharis Publishing is an imprint of Kharis Media LLC. Learn more at
https://www.kharispublishing.com.

Citation

[1] Please add a citation for John C Maxwell's book. The 8 pillars of excellence. Publisher : Struik Inspirational; 1st Edition (January 1, 2012)
ISBN-13: 978-1415313633
ISBN-10: 1415313636

www.ingramcontent.com/pod-product-compliance
Lightning Source LLC
Chambersburg PA
CBHW070547090426
42735CB00013B/3102